THE RAPE OF THE
BEL

A Come

by

BENN W. LEVY

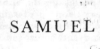

SAMUEL FRENCH

LONDON

NEW YORK TORONTO SYDNEY HOLLYWOOD

THE RAPE OF THE BELT

Produced at the Piccadilly Theatre, London, on the 12th December 1957, with the following cast of characters—

(in the order of their appearance)

HERA	*Veronica Turleigh*
ZEUS	*Nicholas Hannen*
HIPPOBOMENE	*Judith Furse*
THESEUS	*Richard Attenborough*
HERACLES	*John Clements*
ANTIOPE	*Constance Cummings*
DIASTA	*Clare Bradley*
* ANTHEA	*Ann Martin*
HIPPOLYTE	*Kay Hammond*
THALESTRIS	*Susan Richards*

Directed by JOHN CLEMENTS
Décor by MALCOLM PRIDE

SYNOPSIS OF SCENES

PROLOGUE

ACT I

Outside the Palace of Themiscyra

ACT II

SCENE 1   A courtyard inside the Palace. Two hours later
SCENE 2   The same. The next morning

ACT III

SCENE 1   The same. A few minutes later

SCENE 2   The same. A few weeks later

* *This character may be eliminated and the lines spoken by Diasta*

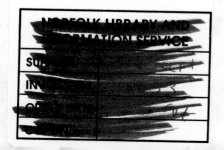

THE RAPE OF THE BELT*

PROLOGUE

SCENE—*The scene is a frontcloth: and is a painted screen curtain depicting, in the manner of Greek vase drawings, a bloody battle between Greeks and ferocious Amazons. About this curtain is a false proscenium arch, Grecian in architecture. High on each side of it is a niche three or four feet high. In one of them, upon a pedestal, there is a marble bust of Hera; in the other there is a pedestal but no bust. Hera is in the niche R and Zeus is in the niche L. The niches can be concealed by gauze curtains. On the face of each curtain is a picture of each god, listening, so that as the action proceeds, the gods are therefore still present, while the actors playing them can retire.*

Before the CURTAIN *rises, the music from a lyre or harp is heard in the darkness.*

When the CURTAIN *rises, the general lighting grows and spots are focused on the niches* R *and* L. HERA *is in place but Zeus is missing.*

HERA.
    Under serene Olympus Atlas holds
    A little ball aloft where nights and days
    Are petering paragraphs, some sadly short,
    Others as sadly long but all of them
    Writ to a final punctuation point.
    Yet, though they string to a tale of little meaning,
    Lacking an end and a beginning, yet,
    They make for gods and goddesses, who bear
    The brunt and inconvenience of eternity,
    Light reading for the bedside.
    This night you too are gods, for you have found
    Promotion in this magic box, a theatre.
    Here you may smile with us at the quaint pains
    Of agonized mankind—whence you have bought
    A fleeting ticket of leave. And you shall skim
    With us a paragraph or two while Time,
    Your bully, lies asleep.

(*There is an arpeggio on the harp*)

                  I am white-armed,
    Ox-eyed, gold-seated Hera. What saith Zeus?

(*There is a long pause*)

---

*N.B. Paragraph 3 on page ii of this Acting Edition regarding photocopying and video-recording should be carefully read.

(*She repeats herself more firmly*)
                    I am white-armed,
Ox-eyed, gold-seated Hera. What saith Zeus?

(*After another silence the* PROMPTER's *voice is faintly heard*)

PROMPTER (*off*)
Under serene Olympus my brave boy . . .
HERA. What?

(*The* PROMPTER *comes forward* L *a step, and is just visible by the proscenium*)

PROMPTER.
Under serene Olympus my brave boy,
Briefly a human and tumultuous . . .

(*The marble head of* ZEUS, *a little damp about the forehead, appears upon the pedestal in the niche* L)

ZEUS. Excuse me.
Under serene Olympus my brave boy . . .

(*The* PROMPTER *withdraws*)

HERA. I'll give you serene Olympus! Where have you been?
ZEUS. Ssh!
Briefly a human and tumultuous,
Sustains his father's honour. Heracles,
My son, the noblest of the multitude
That I have sired . . .
HERA. Where have you been?
ZEUS. My dear, we are not alone
HERA. Who was it this time? Leda, Io, Europa, Semele or some new strumpet?
ZEUS. I'm late. I know I'm late. And I have apologized. I was kept. I had a long way to come and go.
HERA. No doubt. And some baggage to see to.
ZEUS. Dear, *not* before the mortals, please.
HERA. Oh come, Leda may have found you convincing in the guise of a swan and even I, as I blush to recall, once mistook you—more understandably—for a cuckoo; but do not, I beg, attempt to play the ostrich. You cannot gad about earth, sea and sky for thousands of years like an unsated satyr and expect nobody to notice. Sooner or later even *they* ferret out most things. Besides what they surmise or make up is usually truer than what they learn. And they must surmise *some* occupation for you.
ZEUS. True, eternity needs a lot of killing. You would remember that in my favour, if you had more charity.
HERA. Of course I am only a female but am I not eternal, too?
ZEUS. Indeed you are. And I am often puzzled to know what you do with your time.

HERA. Being your wife and sister is scarcely a part-time occupation. But whatever I may do, at least I respect my marriage vows.

ZEUS. We-e-ell—you *did* give birth to Hephaestos, you know—with no assistance that I can recall from me.

HERA. And what does that prove, pray? I trust you're not denying that there's such a thing as virgin birth and has been ever since gods were first invented?

ZEUS (*sceptically*) Well . . .

HERA. Sometimes you sound more like a common atheist than a god.

ZEUS (*mildly deprecating*) Oh no, I hope not.

HERA. And the key word, if I may say so, is common. If you would confine your antics to women of your own class, I should mind far less; but these furtive, squalid caperings with mortals, these secret adventures in a blaze of immortal publicity, are undignified and degrading. Sometimes I think you half *enjoy* the publicity. What after all could be more ill-bred than . . .

ZEUS. Hadn't we better continue, my love? "Under serene Olympus my brave boy . . ."

HERA. That's what I mean. Hercules! Your brave boy! Instead of having the grace, the gentility, to deny his parentage, you are forever boasting of it.

ZEUS. I think it would be far more ill-bred to deny it, my dear. And my son's name is Heracles. Only to Romans and other upstarts is he Hercules.

HERA. But *is* he your son? For all we *know* he is nothing of the kind.

ZEUS. Surely there can be little doubt?

HERA. Simply because you stooped to impersonate his father?

ZEUS. But rather successfully, my dear. After all, his mother took me for Amphitryon and—she took me.

HERA. Is that conclusive?

ZEUS. Ah! You raise a novel legal point. You mean to say, when I borrow Amphitryon's body to woo his wife, is the resulting progeny fathered by the body or by the body's occupant, by the ground-landlord, as it were, or by the tenant? Fascinating. It should keep the lawyers busy.

HERA. I did *not* mean that but, in the absence of a ruling, you could at least have disclaimed the child or kept silent.

ZEUS. You would not let me. If you recall, you raised the Olympian roof-tops with your denunciations.

HERA. What did you expect me to do?

ZEUS. Just what you did, my dear.

HERA. There was a principle involved.

ZEUS. The principle of monogamy? If I am common, are you perhaps being a little parochial?

HERA. Different rules for the sexes—that's what I was objecting to. I tell you I am sick and tired of a Heaven in which goddesses are second-class citizens.

Zeus. My dear, a feminist is a lady who makes the mistake of supposing that the war of the sexes has been lost. Curb your defeatism. It could end in your defeat.

Hera. Could it? You have not yet learned that what a god can do a goddess can do.

Zeus. True, I like to think she would not stoop so low.

Hera. We can dispense with flattery. I know you are convinced that no woman is as wise as Solon, as valorous as Hector or as reasonable as Socrates.

Zeus. I am convinced no man is as pretty as Helen; nor as patient as Penelope.

Hera. Precisely; our function is merely to be decorative—and to wait.

Zeus. Why have you decided that beauty is a second-class virtue and reason a first-class one? Why do you rate patience below valour?

Hera. Can women not be brave?

Zeus. I have never thought otherwise.

Hera. If you *had*, I fancy your boy Heracles will shortly be in a position to disillusion you.

Zeus. Heracles? Explain.

Hera. The play we are to see tonight——

Zeus. Of which we form the somewhat undisciplined prologue . . .

Hera. —will tell the tale of your precious Heracles in conflict with the Amazons.

Zeus. Will he do well?

Hera. Not if I can help it.

Zeus. Oh come, my dear; from now on we are spectators.

Hera. We have our Olympian rights, I hope? If I dislike the way things go, I warn you I shall intervene.

Zeus. Mm. That could be interesting. Well, it would not be the first time you have harassed that long-suffering lad. Being my bastard seems to have its drawbacks as well as its distinction. However—let us proceed then; shall we? " Under serene Olympus my brave boy . . ."

Hera. We have had that more than once already.

Zeus. You are quite right, my dear. Indeed, perhaps it would be well, owing to my unpunctuality and your loquacity . . .

Hera. Mine!

Zeus. Ours—if we were to skip the introductory scene which tells, I understand, how King Eurystheus imposed upon my ill-starred son for his Ninth Labour the task of wresting from proud Queen Antiope her glittering royal belt, most prized possession of her fierce subject Amazons.   Agreed?

Hera. Agreed.

ZEUS. Then let us overleap the journey and arrive at the arrival of the fleet, emerging from the Thracian straits upon the broad Euxine——

(*The sound of the lyre is heard*)

—whereafter, with more sea-miles behind, anchors are cast and, standing upon the prow with gallant Theseus, his good comrade, my Heracles takes his first sight of the enemy stronghold, the beetling city of Themiscyra . . .

The music swells and is augmented by the rhythmic beat of some percussion instrument. The lights on the niches R *and* L *fade and the gauze curtains come down in each niche.*

ACT I

Scene—*Outside the Palace of Themiscyra.*

The entrance to the palace is through double doors L, *approached by three broad steps. Above the entrance is a segment of a vast, circular watch-tower. From the tower, a great wall runs across and down* R. *All the masonry is thick, rude, ancient stone. There is an entrance down* R. *An anvil stands* LC, *with a brazier below it.*

(See the Ground Plan at the end of the Play)

When the Frontcloth *rises, the lights come up and it becomes clear that the percussion instrument we have heard is an enormous sledge-hammer which* Hippobomene, *a blacksmith, is wielding without undue effort upon the anvil. She is repairing a four-foot iron hinge, hot from the brazier, for the palace door. She is a gigantic, powerful-looking woman with short, strong hair and bushy eyebrows, and a brow fiercely knit in concentration. On her sixth blow,* Theseus's *head is raised with extreme caution above the wall up* C. *He bobs down as* Hippobomene *lays down her big hammer on the ground and picks up a smaller hammer. She grasps the hinge in a cloth and deals little blows on the anvil and hinge, humming to herself.* Theseus *reappears, very gingerly raises himself on to the wall, lifts his bow and gauges an aim at Hippobomene's turned back. He feels for an arrow, but finds to his consternation that his quiver is empty. He looks about him, sets his teeth and lowers himself quietly into the garden. He lays down his bow and is about to unbuckle his quiver, when* Hippobomene *straightens herself and looks along the edge of the hinge.* Theseus *pauses.* Hippobomene *takes the hinge to the brazier, lays down her hammer, grips the hinge in a long pair of pincers and puts it into the brazier.* Theseus *lays down his quiver, creeps up behind Hippobomene, reaches stealthily for the large hammer and is about to lift it. Unfortunately, it is too heavy for him. He succeeds in raising it only a few inches from the ground but the thud of its fall is sufficient to alert* Hippobomene, *who swings round and looks down at Theseus with astonishment.*

Hippobomene. Who are you?

(Hippobomene *puts her foot smartly on the shaft of the hammer so that* Theseus's *hand which grips it is pinned rather painfully against the ground*)

Theseus (*sotto voce*) Ouch! Look out!

Hippobomene. Who are you? How on earth did you get up here?

Theseus. Take your foot up. You're pinching me.

Hippobomene (*removing her foot*) Serves you right. Sneaking up here . . .

6

THESEUS. Don't shout. Oo, my knuckles!

HIPPOBOMENE. Why shouldn't I shout? If people come out of the Palace and catch you up here, it will be your own fault. Who *are* you? How did you manage it? How did you get away from the Farm?

THESEUS (*rising and sucking his fingers impatiently*) What farm, for heaven's sake?

HIPPOBOMENE. Don't talk to me like that. Who do you think you are? Show a little respect, if you please. How did you escape? (*With her pliers she touches the sword and dagger at his waist*) And where did you get this rubbish?

THESEUS. Rubbish? I'll show you if it's rubbish. (*He draws and lunges at her*)

(HIPPOBOMENE, *startled and affronted, instinctively whacks his sword with her pliers, and sends it flying from his numbed fingers*)

HIPPOBOMENE. You dreadful little man! What *is* the matter with you? You must be out of your mind. (*She takes a step or two towards him*)

THESEUS (*backing* L) Stay away. I warn you. You may be bigger than I but I'm not without experience of monsters. True, when I slew the Minotaur, my fingers were in working order, but I am not done yet.

HIPPOBOMENE. Don't be so silly. I'm not going to hurt you. You're ill and you must be taken back to the Farm. The vet will attend to you, though I doubt if, after this, you can be made use of in the future. Still, wait here. I'm only going to get help. (*She crosses towards the palace*)

(THESEUS, *as Hippobomene passes him, runs after her and springs on to her back*)

THESEUS. Oh, no, you don't.

(THESEUS *can just reach high enough to wind his arm around* HIPPOBOMENE'S *throat and, by putting forth all his strength, succeeds in dragging her backwards. Unfortunately, he trips over the hammer so that they crash to the ground, still locked, with* HIPPOBOMENE *on top of him. We can almost hear the breath whistling out of his body, but he clings on like the hero he is*)

HIPPOBOMENE (*screaming*) Help! Help! Help! (*She tears at his imprisoning arm, manages to squirm round and ends up kneeling on his head*) Help! Help!

(HERACLES *appears in answer to the hubbub, vaulting on to the broad wall, with his great club over his shoulder. He is a tremendous man, dwarfing even Hippobomene. He has a light-brown beard a little ruddier than his hair, and a muscular face of great beauty and conflicting traits, dominating, sensitive, irascible, sensual, intelligent and sad. He is fully armed and over his clothes a lion-skin, with its head dangling, is slung across one shoulder)*

HERACLES *(swiftly taking in the situation)* I come. Heracles!

(An echo of Heracles' voice is heard in the distance. HERACLES *leaps from the wall, seizes Hippobomene by the belt of her leather apron with one hand, her collar by the other, and swings her to the ground)*

HIPPOBOMENE. Let me be. How dare you! Take your hands off me, will you.

HERACLES. Who strikes at my comrade strikes at me.

HIPPOBOMENE. I didn't strike at him: he struck at me.

(HERACLES releases Hippobomene, gets her to her feet but retains a firm grip on her collar)

HERACLES *(to Theseus)* Is that true? Did you attack this monstrous woman, unprovoked?

(THESEUS attempts to answer but, as air has not yet returned to his lungs, no sounds emerge save a few disconnected sibilants)

What is the matter with you?

(THESEUS' lips move almost noiselessly again)

(He releases Hippobomene) Stay there. If you move, I'll lop your head off. *(He kneels beside Theseus)* What is it, old comrade?

(THESEUS, feeble with suffocation, weakly conveys in dumb show what has happened)

You mean she sat on you?

(THESEUS nods)

But why were you lying down? Here, take a deep breath.

(THESEUS takes a deep breath while HERACLES works his arms wide and high to expand the lungs)

There. Is that better?

THESEUS. Thanks, old fellow. *(He sits up, inhaling deeply)*

HERACLES *(with a step towards the frightened Hippobomene)* Are you a guard?

HIPPOBOMENE. A what?

HERACLES. A guard, woman. What are you?

HIPPOBOMENE. I'm—I am the palace blacksmith and odd-job woman.

HERACLES. Where is your mistress?

HIPPOBOMENE. What?

HERACLES. The queen, woman, the queen. Where is the queen?

HIPPOBOMENE. Inside, I suppose.

HERACLES *(moving up* c) Then go and tell her the lord Heracles is here and begs to be received.

HIPPOBOMENE (*incredulously*) You mean—will she see you?
HERACLES. That's what I said.
HIPPOBOMENE. But of *course* she won't see you. I don't know if I'm on my head or my heels.
HERACLES. If you do not do as you are told, I shall relieve you of all doubt: you will be on your head again. Off with you.

(HIPPOBOMENE *runs up the steps* L, *then stops and turns*)

HIPPOBOMENE. What did you say the name was?
HERACLES. Heracles.
HIPPOBOMENE. Will she have heard of it?
HERACLES. She will be unusual if she hasn't.
HIPPOBOMENE. *I* am unusual.
HERACLES (*shouting*) Be off!

(HIPPOBOMENE *flees into the palace* L, *closing the door behind her*)

(*He crosses and sits on the anvil*) Better?
THESEUS (*feeling his diaphragm*) Yes.
HERACLES. What happened?
THESEUS. These women are dangerous.
HERACLES. We knew that much before we sailed.
THESEUS. I feel a little sick.
HERACLES. Take it easy, old friend.
THESEUS. A hero's life is not all beer and skittles, is it?
HERACLES. We must fulfil our destiny.
THESEUS. Not that I should choose anything else, I suppose, if I had my chance again. Still . . .
HERACLES. What happened?
THESEUS. I tripped on that infernal hammer.
HERACLES. What else?
THESEUS. I had made a careful note of the lie of the land, then I crept on to that wall. No-one had seen me and no-one was in sight still except that confounded blacksmith. And *her* back was turned. I raised my bow. It was only ten yards' range. I could have caught her beautifully, smack between the shoulder blades —couldn't have missed—sitting hippopotamus. I put my hand to my quiver and what do you think? I had forgotten to bring any arrows. Isn't it astonishing?
HERACLES (*rising*) It is more astonishing that you remembered even to bring your quiver. (*He picks up the big heavy hammer, swings it easily and puts it over his shoulder*) But what I *should* like to know is why you slipped away from me.
THESEUS (*rising*) I didn't slip away from you. I lagged behind to take in the topography and make a few mental notes.
HERACLES. Ah, yes. And where did you put them for safe-keeping?
THESEUS. Now, come, old boy. Just because I happened to forget a few arrows . . . (*He picks up his sword*)

(*The harsh sound of trumpets is heard off*)

What's that?

HERACLES. Trumpets. (*He puts the hammer down* R) They're coming. Put back your sword.

THESEUS. Suppose there's trouble?

HERACLES. Already? They don't yet know the purpose of our visit.

THESEUS. They may have guessed. They may be treacherous. I shall not trust them. Dear god of war, I hope I haven't forgotten anything.

(HERACLES *grips his club and looks alertly at the palace door*)

HERACLES. Where is your nerve, man? This isn't like you.

THESEUS (*crossing to Heracles and standing above him*) If you had my sore knuckles . . . I mean, one can't even grip properly. Besides . . .

(*A fanfare of trumpets is heard closer. The palace doors swing open. Another fanfare is heard even closer.*

The QUEEN ANTIOPE *enters from the palace and stands at the top of the steps* L.

DIASTA *and* ANTHEA, *Antiope's attendants, follow her on and stand each side of the doors,* DIASTA *downstage.* ANTIOPE *is a golden beauty, bewitching, radiant, strikingly feminine and dressed in the most becoming taste. She smiles graciously upon her visitors*)

ANTIOPE. How do you do?

THESEUS (*after a dumb-struck moment*) Well, bless me! (*He beams appreciatively*)

ANTIOPE. I should be glad to, but I am qualified only to offer you a welcome, my lord.

THESEUS. Very kind, I am sure.

ANTIOPE. You come from a far land?

THESEUS (*moving* C) From Greece, your highness.

ANTIOPE. Ah, yes: where, I see, it is customary to visit one's friends with a drawn sword.

THESEUS (*hastily sheathing his sword*) No, no, your highness, I assure you . . .

ANTIOPE. Diasta, a seat, if you please.

(DIASTA *and* ANTHEA *exit to the palace*)

Are you the lord Heracles?

THESEUS (*eagerly*) No, I am Theseus, son of Aegeus—royal, you understand. My father was king of Athens; my grandfather was Pittheus. No doubt you have heard of him.

ANTIOPE. I am sure I should have. You must forgive Themiscyra for being so remote.

THESEUS. Of course, of course; don't mention it.

(ANTIOPE *descends the steps and crosses to Heracles*)

ANTIOPE. The message mentioned the name of Heracles. Is this he? He is very silent.

(THESEUS *moves to* L *of Antiope*)

HERACLES. In the presence of great beauty I fall silent. (*This is said gravely, not as a courtier's compliment*)

ANTIOPE. Thank you. We have a bond already. You, too, have beauty. It is a valuable equipment, isn't it?

HERACLES. In women, madam.

ANTIOPE. Curious, here it is valued more highly in men. This is an occasion of unusual interest for us. Male visitors are almost without precedent. So naturally Hippobomene was unaccustomed and surprised at being attacked. You must excuse her.

THESEUS. Well, you mustn't think—I mean, it was the purest accident. You mustn't think we make a practice of attacking women.

ANTIOPE. That is very reassuring. I did hope you were not given to any practice so—so imprudent.

(DIASTA *and* ANTHEA *enter from the palace, carrying an elegant bench which they set down* LC. ANTIOPE *crosses to the bench and sits, mildly surprised that* THESEUS *should be gallantly helping her*)

THESEUS. Allow me.

ANTIOPE. Thank you. What a charming custom. Here we reserve it for the very old. Diasta, seats for the gentlemen.

HERACLES. No, thank you, madam. We are well as we are.

(DIASTA *and* ANTHEA *go up the steps* L *and stand each side of the door,* DIASTA *downstage*)

THESEUS. We are rough, hard-living warriors, your highness, and would as soon stand as sit. (*He crosses to the steps* L, *sits and beams at Antiope*)

ANTIOPE. As you please. I gather from some of your remarks that Greece is not a matriarchy?

THESEUS (*roaring with laughter*) Matriarchy! Oh, that's very good! No, Greece is not a matriarchy.

ANTIOPE. Themiscyra is.

THESEUS. You don't say so. Yes, well, I suppose it would be, wouldn't it? I mean, no men, you know, and all that. (*He rises and moves to* L *of the bench*) Tell me, one thing has always puzzled me— how exactly do you manage to—well, how shall I put it . . .?

ANTIOPE. I was about to ask whether you would not care for some refreshment after your journey.

THESEUS. Well, since you mention it . . .

HERACLES. No, thank you, madam. We must not make our mission even harder than it is.

ANTIOPE. That has an ominous sound, my lord. Shall we dispense with the preliminaries? What has brought you here?

HERACLES. I will tell you. (*He pauses and puts his club against the wall up* RC) I trust it will not seem to you unduly trivial; or better perhaps that it *should* seem so. It is less likely to cause contention between us. (*He pauses*)

ANTIOPE. Go on, my lord.

THESEUS (*to Antiope*) It *is* a little tricky.

HERACLES. Theseus, please!

(ANTIOPE *looks from one to the other, wondering*)

Madam, we seek a—a favour from you. I hope it will not seem to you too—exacting.

ANTIOPE. I am sure I shall seek to grant it.

(*There is a pause.* THESEUS *crosses behind the bench to* R *of it*)

THESEUS. Go on; tell her, old man.

HERACLES. I am trying to tell her! Madam, you have a belt.

(ANTIOPE *looks down at her waist and up again enquiringly*)

No, not at the moment but—but somewhere—about the place.

(ANTIOPE *begins to doubt his sanity*)

Madam, I beg you not to look as though you were concerned about my health.

THESEUS. No, he's perfectly sane, really. I've never seen him like this. It must be you.

HERACLES. Theseus, be silent! (*He wipes his damp forehead*) Madam, if report be true, you have a belt, a royal belt, a sacred belt, a famous belt . . .

ANTIOPE. Yes, my lord?

HERACLES. The fact is, I regret to say—the fact is we—we have come for it.

ANTIOPE. Come for it?

HERACLES. I am afraid that—is what I said.

ANTIOPE (*incredulously*) You mean you—want my belt?

HERACLES. We do, madam.

ANTIOPE. Forgive me if I am slow, but—but what for?

HERACLES. What for? Yes. A legitimate question. Er—it is not I exactly that wants it: it is Eurystheus.

ANTIOPE. Who is Eurystheus?

HERACLES. He is a worm, my lady; the king of Argos and a worm.

ANTIOPE. What made you servant to a worm?

THESEUS. The mighty Heracles is no man's servant.

HERACLES. Thank you but she is right. I serve him: that is my shame. But it is a long story and I shall not weary you with it.

THESEUS (*to Antiope*) It is really very simple. He was put to serve Eurystheus as a penance and given twelve extremely tricky labours to perform. This is number eight.

HERACLES. Nine.

ANTIOPE. A penance for what?

THESEUS. Well, the fact is he is cursed with the most vile and violent temper. In a twinkling it can turn him into a raging maniac, and as for controlling it, he is utterly incapable . . .

HERACLES. It is a lie! (*He seizes Theseus by the throat and savagely shakes him*) How dare you lie! You know quite well I have conquered my temper.

(*The* WOMEN *cower*)

You know I have complete control. (*He swings Theseus round to his right*)

(ANTIOPE *rises and retreats up the steps* L)

THESEUS (*half choked*) Yes, my dear chap, I know you have. I was speaking of long ago.

(HERACLES *releases* THESEUS *who retreats down* R)

HERACLES (*crossing above the bench to the steps* L) Long ago, madam, I had the misfortune to kill my dear wife when I was cross.

THESEUS (*feeling his neck*) And your dear children.

HERACLES (*with a step towards Theseus*) All right, all right.

THESEUS. And a couple of dear nieces.

HERACLES. All right.

THESEUS (*moving up* R) And Linos, your tutor. Not to mention . . .

HERACLES (*crossing to Theseus*) That will *do*, thank you. (*He pauses*) Are you in a position to cast a stone? Who killed his father?

THESEUS. Now come, old fellow; I didn't kill him exactly. It was purely an accident. (*He crosses above the bench to Antiope*) You see, I was coming home from one of my early exploits, which was particularly tricky, and my father hadn't wanted me to go. I insisted so he gave way; but he asked me to hoist white sails if I returned safely, instead of the black ones with which we had set out. Well, the fact is I clean forgot to change them and when the poor old fellow saw the black sails coming across the bay, he was so upset he threw himself off a cliff. It was very unfortunate but the purest slip.

ANTIOPE. That *was* unfortunate.

HERACLES. Tell them about Ariadne; how you forgot her, also.

THESEUS (*crossing above the bench to Heracles*) No, really, my dear chap. Just because I happened to mention your temper, you don't need to rake up every tiny mistake I've ever made.

ANTIOPE (*coming down the steps and standing below the bench*) Please, gentlemen, do not start brawling again.

HERACLES. Brawling?

ANTIOPE. Well, quarrelling. You have established beyond dispute that you are both in your own different ways—formidable men. Nevertheless, to return to the subject of the belt, much as I should like to show you every hospitality, this particular favour is one that I am quite unable to grant.

HERACLES (*moving to* R *of Antiope*) Is that final?

ANTIOPE. I am *very* sorry. (*She sits on the bench*)

THESEUS (*peering round Heracles*) We would consider buying it, of course.

ANTIOPE. My lord, a buyer without a seller is as incomplete as . . .

HERACLES. As a woman without a man.

ANTIOPE. Or as a seller without a buyer.

THESEUS. She means as a man without a woman. Very true. We've been at sea for weeks and it seems like years. (*He moves down* R)

HERACLES. Thank you. You need not dot the "i's" for us.

THESEUS. I'm sorry, I'm sure.

ANTIOPE. Do not be sorry, my lord. I would willingly meet your suggestion and still more willingly present the thing to your friend here as it seems it would make him happy; but it has for us an especial significance, a kind of constitutional significance.

HERACLES. You mean it is a symbol.

ANTIOPE. That and more. It corresponds, I suppose, to the crown in other lands. Historical sentiment has hallowed it and it has great beauty as well as intrinsic value. It is a national asset. Now if a sovereign, succumbing to pressure or to her own whim, were to surrender the crown jewels to the first thug or footpad who demanded them, she would suffer such a loss in popularity as might have the direst practical consequences.

THESEUS (*with a step forward*) Madam, are you likening Heracles to a thug?

ANTIOPE. I? I hope I shall never be guilty of so direct a discourtesy. (*She looks at Heracles*) On the contrary, I am sure he is a most high-minded warrior. But you could not envy me the task of explaining the distinction to my simple subjects.

HERACLES (*stepping close to Antiope*) It is true I am a warrior, madam, high-minded or otherwise, but I had hoped on this occasion to lay aside my trade.

ANTIOPE. I hear what you are saying, my lord.

HERACLES. Must you persist in your refusal?

ANTIOPE. Alas, my lord, I must.

HERACLES (*unhappily*) Then you leave—you leave me no alternative to war.

Antiope (*after a pause*) It is a tremendous monosyllable, my lord. Can you not find a smaller one?

Heracles (*moving up* C; *sorrowfully*) I am cursed with a limited vocabulary.

Antiope. Then we have met a crisis. I must send for the Queen. Diasta, do you mind?

(Diasta *and* Anthea *exit to the palace*)

Theseus. The Queen?

Antiope. Oh, had you not heard? There are two of us; my sister and myself. My own province is Home Affairs: my sister is Foreign Secretary and Minister of Defence.

Theseus. Minister of Defence? A woman? (*He strolls up* RC *towards Heracles*) Oh, yes, of course: you have no alternative, have you?

(Heracles *withdraws to the wall up* C *and looks ruminatively seaward*)

Antiope (*smiling*) Yes, having no men to work for us, we have no alternative to working for ourselves. In Greece, I see, it is different.

(Heracles *turns and moves down* R)

Theseus (*crossing to Antiope*) Oh, yes: our women never work; naturally—except of course for a little cooking—and washing—and cleaning and mending and weaving—and, of course, nursing; oh, and agricultural work, reaping and binding and hoeing and weeding and digging and a few things of that sort.

Antiope. But otherwise no work.

Theseus. Not a stroke.

Antiope. Is so much leisure good for them?

Theseus. Well, we sometimes wonder. Tell me something; when you say you have no men, does that mean you have no men even for—how shall I put it? The question was on the tip of my tongue some minutes ago.

Antiope. I noticed that it was: how do we perpetuate ourselves.

Theseus (*with a step back; nodding*) You put it beautifully. (*He pauses then takes a step towards Antiope*) Well, how do you?

Antiope. We keep a small handful of men for the purpose.

Theseus. Really? I haven't seen any.

Antiope. Oh, no; they are not allowed loose, of course. They are kept at what we call the Stud Farm. It is at Synope, a tiny peninsula to the north; very convenient as it is difficult for them to escape. The neck of land is guarded by a high wall, so we have little trouble.

Theseus. Good God! You *keep* them there? How do they live?

Antiope. Oh, in sheds: quite nice sheds, very hygienic. We

wash the men regularly and feed them on a fairly scientific diet and of course every so often, whenever a woman wishes to procreate, she pays a visit to the Farm.

THESEUS (*with a step back*)   But this is horrible!

ANTIOPE. No, no; believe me, it all works very simply and naturally in practice.

THESEUS. Then that's the farm your blacksmith was raving about? She thought I had escaped.

ANTIOPE. Poor Hippobomene. An understandable mistake.

(*A fanfare of trumpets is heard off.*

QUEEN HIPPOLYTE *enters from the palace, and stands at the top of the steps* L. *She is a golden beauty, bewitching, radiant, strikingly feminine and dressed in the most becoming taste. Her outer garment, however, is evidently the ancient forerunner of a negligee. She is extremely sleepy and somewhat startled by the trumpets.* ANTIOPE *rises and moves behind the bench.* HERACLES *moves down to* L *of Theseus.* DIASTA *and* ANTHEA *follow Hippolyte on and stand each side of the door*)

HIPPOLYTE. What on earth's that noise about?

ANTIOPE (*moving to the steps*)   Darling, this, a little unexpectedly, is a state occasion.

HIPPOLYTE (*coming down the steps and standing below the bench*) I thought it must be something if I have to be rooted out of my bed at this barbaric hour: and with trumpets. (*She notices the men*) What on earth are these?

ANTIOPE (*moving down* L)   These are the lords Heracles and Theseus: my sister Hippolyte.

(HERACLES *and* THESEUS *salute by slapping their right fists on their hearts*)

THESEUS (*devastated by Hippolyte's beauty*)   Delighted to meet you, absolutely.

HIPPOLYTE (*puzzled and somewhat offended*)   But these are men.

ANTIOPE. I know appearances are against them but, although they are men by gender, I understand they are heroes by profession.

HIPPOLYTE (*turning to Antiope*)   But what on earth are they doing up here? Why aren't they at the Farm?

THESEUS (*with a step forward*)   It is an interesting idea; if you would accompany me, your highness.

HIPPOLYTE (*sharply*)   Quiet!

(THESEUS *is taken aback*)

Speak when you are spoken to. Antiope, has Themiscyra gone off its head while I've been sleeping? Will you explain . . .

HERACLES (*crossing to Hippolyte; containing his indignation*)   I will explain . . .

HIPPOLYTE. I did not speak to you. I . . .

HERACLES (*booming*) Quiet!

HIPPOLYTE. Good heavens! (*She sits on the bench*)

HERACLES. I shall expect civility or you will receive none. My friend and I . . .

ANTIOPE (*crossing above the bench to R of it*) My lord, will you allow me? Hippolyte, these gentlemen are not fugitives from the Farm. They come from a far country where, believe it or not, the male, it seems, holds quite a dominant position. His status is no whit inferior to the female's, so what you must take for impertinence is to them quite normal behaviour.

HIPPOLYTE. Oh. Nevertheless they are not at home now: they must be taught to leave their native eccentricities behind them.

ANTIOPE (*her face signalling a warning*) That is not all. They are here upon a mission—(*she turns winningly to Heracles*) may I say a mission disagreeable to all four of us?

HERACLES. You would certainly be speaking for me.

ANTIOPE (*turning to Hippolyte*) It seems they are under some compulsion to demand from us the royal girdle. When I refused, they spoke—in the most gentlemanly fashion, of course—they spoke of war.

HIPPOLYTE. But this is absurd!

(ANTIOPE *moves up* C)

They may be men but after all they *are* fully grown. A war about a belt?

HERACLES. It is not of my seeking. I should prefer to depart with it in peace.

HIPPOLYTE. Well, that is cool, I must say.

ANTIOPE (*moving above the bench*) I am afraid they are quite serious. Already they have assaulted poor Hippobomene.

HIPPOLYTE. They haven't! Poor Hippo!

HERACLES (*moving* C) We are so serious, madam, that it is time we made the necessary arrangements. As Minister for War, will you confer with me?

HIPPOLYTE. What about?

HERACLES. Where do you suggest the contest should take place? Have you a suitable battlefield? And what hour would be convenient for you?

HIPPOLYTE. Well, I suppose I *am* awake? Believe me, sir, this is not a very good idea.

ANTIOPE. It will only end in tears.

HERACLES (*moving up* C) Thank you for your warning, madam, but it does not alarm us, even though we know well your reputation.

HIPPOLYTE. Have you heard of our ever having been defeated?

HERACLES. On the contrary: it is common knowledge that you

never have. But, madam, nor have we. (*He pauses, moves to* L *of Theseus, folds his arms and draws himself up ominously*)

(THESEUS *folds his arms and also draws himself up*)

I am waiting.

(*The* QUEENS *look at each other*)

ANTIOPE (*moving to* R *of the bench*) My lord Heracles; this is the second proposal you have made to me in our brief acquaintance, and the second that I must refuse. You will be thinking us very disobliging. (*She sits* R *of Hippolyte on the bench*)

HERACLES. I do not think I understand. Just what are you refusing

ANTIOPE. To accept your invitation to a war.

THESEUS. Wha-at?

HIPPOLYTE. We like you far too much.

THESEUS. Well, that's all very well . . .

HERACLES. But can we not fight without rancour? We are not savages.

ANTIOPE. Even the proposal to slaughter each other in a civilized way does not attract me. Forgive us.

HIPPOLYTE. Now let us talk of something else.

HERACLES. But—but—I really don't know what to say. You are creating an extremely awkward situation.

ANTIOPE. Oh, don't say that. You will make me feel badly.

THESEUS. But can't you understand? We don't want to press you, of course . . .

HERACLES (*moving* C) You see, you can't both refuse a challenge and refuse to surrender.

ANTIOPE. But we have.

HERACLES. But you can't.

THESEUS. It's against the rules.

HIPPOLYTE. It's not against our rules.

HERACLES. Theseus is right: there is not a single precedent. I mean what are *we* supposed to do? Really, I do wish you would reconsider . . .

ANTIOPE (*after a pause*) Darling, shall we be candid with them?

HIPPOLYTE (*after a pause*) Do you think we ought?

ANTIOPE. No, but they have behaved rather nicely and they *are* very worried.

HIPPOLYTE. And dreadfully persistent.

ANTIOPE. It might be best.

HIPPOLYTE. Very well.

ANTIOPE (*after a pause*) Gentlemen, we cannot agree to fight you—and believe me, if it would give you any pleasure, there is no-one we would rather fight than you—but we cannot do so for a simple reason. It is because . . .

HERACLES (*after a pause*) Because what?

ANTIOPE. Because we never fight.

HERACLES. Never fight?

THESEUS. Why ever not?

HIPPOLYTE. Well, I suppose because we think it's silly.

HERACLES (*taking umbrage*) Madam, are you trying to pick a quarrel? (*He moves down* C)

HIPPOLYTE. No, of course not.

HERACLES (*with a step towards the Queens*) Then I will thank you to keep a civil tongue in your head.

ANTIOPE. We cannot fight you, my lord, because, as we have said, it would only end in tears—in our tears. If we were fortunate, we might score tears on your side, too; a few tears from a few of your wives and mothers. This seems to us an insufficient prize. We cannot fight for the satisfaction of making a few strange women weep. We cannot fight, moreover—to be blunt with you —because we should very certainly be beaten.

HERACLES. But, if report be true, you have never lost a battle yet?

ANTIOPE. It *is* true, but for a very simple reason: it is because we have never fought one.

HERACLES. But—but . . . (*He looks at Theseus*)

THESEUS. Well, really!

HERACLES. But—but—but—but . . .

HIPPOLYTE. I hope we haven't shocked you.

ANTIOPE. Diasta, bring my lord a drink: he is looking pale.

(HERACLES *moves up* L *and motions the Attendants not to trouble*)

HERACLES. No, no; I am quite well. All this is a little surprising that's all.

THESEUS. Surprising? It's dumbfounding.

HERACLES. I thought you said your sister was Minister for War?

HIPPOLYTE. So I am.

ANTIOPE. In fact I said she was Minister of Defence.

HERACLES (*crossing to* L; *impatiently*) Yes, yes; we all call it that these days.

HIPPOLYTE. But ours is a Ministry of Defence with a difference.

THESEUS. I bet it is.

ANTIOPE. In practice it has always been more a Ministry of Propaganda.

HIPPOLYTE. For generations, potential enemies have feared to attack us because of our reputation.

ANTIOPE. The only campaign we have ever embarked upon is a whispering campaign.

HIPPOLYTE. And let nobody underrate it.

ANTIOPE. As soon as one story is well under way, another has been concocted to follow it.

HIPPOLYTE. It seems that nothing is too wild for masculine credulity.

(HERACLES *and* THESEUS *look at each other*)

ANTIOPE. Take, for example, our supposed habit of pectorectomy.

HERACLES. Pectorectomy?

HIPPOLYTE. Yes; surely you have heard that we all amputate our right breasts so as to further our skill with the bow and arrow?

HERACLES. I had heard so, indeed.

ANTIOPE. We don't, you know.

HIPPOLYTE. Isn't it a preposterous story? Oh, dear, I've always enjoyed that one.

ANTIOPE. Our great-aunt Euphemia invented that.

HIPPOLYTE. She was full of little wheezes.

ANTIOPE. She designed those vases and winejars with the preposterous drawings on them, remember?

HIPPOLYTE. Strictly for export only.

ANTIOPE. You must have seen some of them.

HERACLES. We have indeed.

HIPPOLYTE. With pictures of Amazons in battle——

ANTIOPE. —cutting off people's heads with a meat axe——

HIPPOLYTE. —poking their eyes out——

ANTIOPE. —making the most ferocious faces . . .

HIPPOLYTE. And, my dear, the clothes . . .

ANTIOPE. And those hats . . .

HIPPOLYTE. I mean, as if any woman . . .

ANTIOPE. Do you remember . . .?

HIPPOLYTE. Dear old Aunt Feemy. No, don't, darling. We mustn't get carried away. (*She wipes her eyes*) We can hardly expect them to enjoy our family jokes. But you must see, dear man, that if it's war you're after, you've come to the wrong address.

ANTIOPE (*overcoming her giggles*) We are extremely sorry; really we are. But we have a saying here; that you cannot expect the leopardess to change her spots. (*She has another fit of giggles*)

THESEUS (*turning away down* R) Well, I wish I knew what the joke was.

HIPPOLYTE (*rising and crossing to Theseus*) Please forgive us; we shouldn't have got the giggles.

THESEUS. Dear lady, I could forgive you worse than that.

ANTIOPE (*to Heracles*) My lord, pray do not be so glum. We intended no discourtesy.

HERACLES (*moving to* L *of the bench*) I am not glum. I am merely bewildered. What makes all this so hard to understand is—(*he shrugs*) a score of things.

ANTIOPE. Tell me.

HERACLES. Well, at home, you see, women are every bit as ferocious and bloodthirsty as the men—perhaps more so. That is one reason why your reputation was so easy to accept.

ANTIOPE. But, as I understand it, where you come from, women take their cue from men. That is a topsy-turvy state of affairs which is bound to produce topsy-turvy results.

HERACLES (*indicating the building*) For another thing, why is your city constructed like a fortress? (*He crosses above the bench to* R *of it*) Is that, too, propaganda?

ANTIOPE. Oh, we did not build it. We merely modernized it.

HIPPOLYTE. Not the outside, of course. (*She crosses to Antiope*) It was built by an ancient war-like race with such a pathological passion for bravery that they apparently succeeded in destroying even themselves. At any rate, when our ancestors came upon the place it was deserted.

ANTIOPE. Of course, from the propaganda point of view it was quite a useful little windfall.

HIPPOLYTE. And the thick walls make it nice and warm in winter.

ANTIOPE. We have a museum, too, which serves the same useful purpose. It was originally an armoury.

HIPPOLYTE. And it is crammed with the most gruesome weapons.

ANTIOPE. We still call it the Armoury, of course.

HIPPOLYTE. And, needless to say, if we do get any stray travellers, they are always shown it.

ANTIOPE (*sympathetically*) My lord, we have distressed you. It was not my intention. Perhaps it would ease you if we left you to talk it all over with your friend? (*She rises*)

HERACLES. You are very sensitive, madam. I should indeed be glad of a word with him.

ANTIOPE (*moving up* LC) Then I shall go about my morning's work. (*She goes up the steps*)

HIPPOLYTE (*joining Antiope at the top of the steps*) And I shall go and take my bath. All this has exhausted me.

ANTIOPE. You will stay to lunch, won't you?

HERACLES. Oh, thank you. You are very kind.

ANTIOPE. Diasta; two extra for lunch.

(HIPPOLYTE *and* ANTIOPE *exit to the palace.*
DIASTA *and* ANTHEA *follow them off*)

THESEUS (*crossing to the steps* L *and looking after the Queens*) Exquisite!

HERACLES. What are you talking about?

THESEUS. The second one. Hippolyte. I must say she really is— and I don't care if I do use poetical, high-flown language— she really is—my type.

HERACLES. My friend, we are in a pickle.

THESEUS. Are we, old man?

HERACLES. You heard what they said: they won't surrender and they won't fight. (*He sits on the bench*) Could *anything* be more awkward?

THESEUS. I don't see why. (*He sits on the downstage corner of the steps* L) Won't-fight must be made to fight.

HERACLES. They don't know how.

THESEUS. So much the worse for them, I should have thought. In those circumstances they are very foolish to defy us.

HERACLES. I am not so sure. How can we start cutting up a pack of unarmed and very charming ladies who have offered no provocation and don't know a sword from a skewer? (*He rises and crosses to* R) If you can do that in cold blood, you are a better man than I am. No wonder they are not in the least alarmed.

THESEUS. Well, of course, if we *have* to start a massacre we should do it as chivalrously as possible, I admit. I can't see your problem. After all, we expected a tough campaign; instead of a fortress and a long siege, dreary and dangerous, we are confronted with a house of cards, delightful to look at and utterly defenceless. Victory is certain and the spoils delectable: business combined with pleasure, I should have said. Frankly, I've never enjoyed an exploit more.

(HERACLES *sits on the anvil, picks up the small hammer and idly plays with it*)

If Eurystheus has any more labours up his sleeve for you like this, take me with you. After all, it's pleasanter than cleaning out those filthy Augean Stables, isn't it? (*He rises and crosses slowly to Heracles*) What's worrying you, old chap? What are we waiting for? Don't tell me you're infatuated?

HERACLES. Certainly not.

THESEUS. Well, she means you to be, you know; that Antiope. I could see that with half an eye.

HERACLES (*interested*) Do you think so?

THESEUS. I may be slow, but I was not born yesterday. You watch out.

HERACLES. What do you mean?

THESEUS. I mean they may not be as defenceless as I said; at least not that one. Did you ever hear of Samson and Delilah?

HERACLES. No.

THESEUS. It's a tale an old traveller from Mesopotamia told me once. Not very new. You know, a strong man weakened by a woman's wiles.

HERACLES. I fancy she is too proud for that—and correspondingly more dangerous.

THESEUS. I say! Then you admit it?

HERACLES. All right, I admit it. (*He rises and crosses below Theseus to* C)

Theseus. I say, this is serious. You *must* watch out.

Heracles. I must and I shall. Conquering my heart may be the heaviest labour of them all, but I have not failed yet, have I? (*He moves* LC)

Theseus (*crossing to* C) Never let the heart get mixed up in a love-affair, old boy: it can spoil everything. That must be why she is defying us. She thinks you're easy. The sooner you show her otherwise, the better. You must see that?

Heracles (*putting a foot up on the first step*) Unfortunately, I have seen it already. But that is only half the problem. What we have still to solve is how in the world are we to start slaughtering these disarming people who won't oblige us by defending themselves. (*He turns to Theseus*)

Theseus. Well, if you ask me, we took the wrong line. We must provoke them. How does one usually provoke an adversary to fight? You don't go down on your knees and beg him to. You strike him in the face with a glove.

(Heracles *looks sceptically at Theseus for a moment, then takes a glove from his belt*)

Heracles (*tossing the glove to Theseus*) Have a go.

(Theseus *catches the glove*)

Theseus. Why me, old boy?

Heracles (*crossing to Theseus*) Division of labour. You shall use the glove; mine is the harder task of resisting Antiope.

Theseus. I say, really! I mean, after all this *is* your labour. I only came along to help.

Heracles. Then help.

Theseus (*grumbling*) It doesn't seem to me quite fair. Still, if you do your bit properly, I may not be needed. Make her take us a little more seriously. Tell her who you are. Make her realize that she is the one who's up a gum-tree, not we. At present we're all behaving as though it were the other way about. I don't know how it happened. Tell her who you are.

(Antiope *enters from the palace*)

Oh.

Antiope. Excuse my interrupting, but do you both like oysters? I was ordering lunch.

Theseus. I do.

Heracles. So do I.

Antiope. Good. The ones we get from Synope are particularly fine. You shall try them. Make you a big strong boy. (*She turns to go*)

Theseus (*with a step towards Antiope; interrupting her indignantly*) Madam, you are talking to Heracles.

Heracles. That will do, old friend.

ANTIOPE (*turning*) Did I say something I shouldn't?

HERACLES (*to Theseus*) Leave us. Your turn comes later.

THESEUS. Very well, but—but tell her who you are. Be firm.

(THESEUS *crosses and exits* R)

ANTIOPE. That was a strange remark.

HERACLES. My comrade, the lord Theseus, who is sometimes more penetrating than he seems, believes that you underrate your predicament, madam.

ANTIOPE. Meaning that I underrate you, my lord. He is wrong. You are my predicament and I do not underrate it. I merely like it.

HERACLES (*bracing himself against the compliment*) We may be thinking on different planes. I am speaking to you now as a soldier, not as a human being.

ANTIOPE (*coming down the steps*) I appreciate the distinction and must keep it in mind.

HERACLES. As a man you may be right in thinking me malleable; but as a warrior, it is only fair to advise you, I am implacable. This is a distant land. News of the world, of our world, may not reach here easily but, believe me, we have had many opponents, both my lord Theseus and myself, who could testify that we are not easily deflected—if they were alive to do so.

ANTIOPE. I see. You have destroyed your references, as it were. Well, I can take them on trust.

HERACLES. I am not joking, madam.

ANTIOPE. I am sorry to hear it.

HERACLES. Have you heard of the Nemean lion, madam?

ANTIOPE. One of your references? No; tell me. (*She sits on the bench*)

HERACLES. I should like to. It was no ordinary lion. Its father was the giant Typhon and its mother, I believe, the serpent Echidna. It roamed the forests of Argolis undisturbed and its hide was invulnerable to the weapons of man. I sought it out.

ANTIOPE. Oh? Why?

HERACLES. To slay it, madam.

ANTIOPE. Yes, of course.

HERACLES. I found it in a glade, newly returned from the hunt, its jaws and even its mane dripping with fresh blood. It saw me and roared. My arrows broke on its breast. It leapt. I struck it in mid-air with my club. Before it could recover I seized it by the throat and choked it for what seemed an eternal hour until it died.

ANTIOPE. Well, well. And is that its fur?

HERACLES. Its skin? No, this belonged to another lion.

ANTIOPE. That one you bought?

HERACLES. No, madam; I took it from its owner, a more normal beast than the Nemean monster—large, of course, but more normal. It was nothing really, but this was an early exploit. I was barely out of school. I found it on Mount Cythaeron.

Antiope. Cythaeron.

Heracles. On the borders of Megara.

Antiope. My geography is terrible. Tell me more.

Heracles. Did you ever hear of Erginos?

Antiope. No.

Heracles. He was king of the Minyans. I met his messengers on their way to collect an annual tribute from Thebes.

Antiope. Oh, yes?

Heracles. I removed their ears.

Antiope. Dear me.

Heracles. And their noses.

Antiope. Won't you sit down?

Heracles. And returned them empty-handed. It meant war, of course.

Antiope. Of course.

Heracles. So I raised a band of valiant friends to oppose the Minyan host. They were three thousand to our thirty. But we caught them in a narrow pass and slaughtered them at will.

Antiope. And Erginos?

Heracles. I killed him. Then there was Elatos, the centaur. I was dining with his brother Pholos . . .

Antiope. How you can remember all the names . . . !

Heracles (*doggedly*) And insisted on his serving me from a jar of wine that he particularly treasured. He was unwilling but I was adamant.

Antiope. His wine, my belt. Go on.

(Heracles *by now is sweating a little at the temples, but sticks gallantly to his guns*)

Heracles. Finally, fearing a quarrel, he agreed. But Elatos and the other centaurs got wind of it and protested. I drove them back with burning brands and pursued them with poisoned arrows across Malea. As for Elatos . . .

Antiope. You killed him.

Heracles. I did. Then there was Diomedes of Thrace . . .

Antiope. You killed him.

Heracles. Yes, madam. And—and the giant Porphyrion . . .

Antiope. It is quite a list.

Heracles. I am barely at the beginning.

Antiope. Go on: you tell it all so charmingly.

(*There is a silence during which* Heracles *turns away down* R)

Heracles (*quietly*) Madam, I know what you are thinking. Sometimes I think the same: but I put aside such thoughts, for they would hamstring action. A man of action must act or he is nothing.

Antiope (*changing her mood with his*) Being is acting.

Heracles. Then is not acting being?

Antiope. Sometimes, I think, only a substitute for being, a flight from being. I should have judged you good enough simply —to be.

Heracles. It is a flattering picture. I am tempted to aspire to it. It is disturbing here: disturbing. Not only your beauty but your words. (*He crosses below the bench to* lc) Do not enchant me, I pray. My old friend Odysseus had a taste of that. Do not enchant me, for I have work to do, even though—who knows—it be foolish work.

Antiope. Do you fear enchantment?

Heracles. I know I am on the rim of it. If I could enchant you in return, I should be lost.

Antiope. You are safe, my lord. I am unversed in men. The few I have known are slaves. You are the first who is a master: and that I like. And you I like. But we live simple lives here, lives that are unenchanted, uncomplicated, serene, lives that are without—without . . .

Heracles. Romance?

Antiope. Is that the word? It is new to me; even the word. So you see . . .

Heracles. Do you not love?

Antiope. Oh, yes, we love. We do so largely, broadly; we do so, I think, as a matter of course, like breathing. Perhaps because we do not hate.

Heracles. You are a mine of dangerous thoughts. I could not fight without hate: which is to say, I could not live without it. As Theseus told you, my wine is anger; and I am a drunkard.

Antiope. Poor my lord!

(Theseus *enters* r. Heracles, *when he sees Theseus, moves up* c)

Theseus. Well, did you tell her?

Heracles. What? Ye-es—er—yes.

Theseus. Good. Then you don't need me. Or do you?

Heracles. It could do no harm.

Theseus. Very well. Is she ready for me?

Heracles. I should think more than ready.

Antiope. Are you speaking of me?

Theseus (*crossing to* r *of the bench*) We are, your highness. (*He swings the glove a little*) You see, it is like this. The difficulty so far has been to get to grips, to bring things to an issue. (*He tries to hit Antiope but cannot*)

(Heracles *moves down* r *and watches Theseus*)

I imagine my friend has been explaining to you that he is hardly a man to trifle with, so . . .

(HIPPOLYTE *enters from the palace.*

THALESTRIS *accompanies her. She is a stout, comfortable, elderly lady; the ideal nurse, matron or grandmother*)

THALESTRIS (*standing at the top of the steps*) Antiope, could you spare me a few moments to . . . (*She breaks off at the strange sight of two men*) Oh!

ANTIOPE. It is all right, Thalestris. These gentlemen are our friends. My lords Heracles and Theseus, may I present Thalestris, the Minister of Maternity.

HERACLES. Your servant.

(THESEUS *looks interrogatively at Heracles before he bows.* THALESTRIS *regards them for a puzzled moment, then shrugs*)

THALESTRIS. Friends. Gentlemen. Well, I suppose I am old-fashioned.

HIPPOLYTE. Don't worry, dear. It's rather fun. (*She comes down the steps to* L *of the bench. To Antiope*) Darling, Melanippe is asking for you. Could you see her for a minute?

ANTIOPE (*rising*) Yes, of course; is anything wrong?

THALESTRIS. No, no; nothing at all. But she is expecting her baby some time today and in the circumstances this time—well, naturally, she is a little bit on edge.

ANTIOPE. I am not surprised. (*She turns to the men*) Will you excuse me? Melanippe is a daughter of Hippobomene's, whom I think you met. And we are very fond of both of them. Normally, of course, we shouldn't be anxious, but this is her fifth pregnancy and it happens that the other four ended rather tragically. (*She crosses to the steps* L *and goes up them*)

THESEUS (*politely*) Oh, I'm sorry. Stillborn?

ANTIOPE (*turning on the top step*) No, no. All boys.

(ANTIOPE *exits to the palace.*

THALESTRIS *follows her off*)

THESEUS (*indignantly*) Well, really! (*He moves up* C)

(HERACLES *bursts out laughing*)

(*He moves down to Heracles*) Well, what on earth are you laughing at?

HERACLES. I don't know. It must be the woman in me.

THESEUS. I don't understand, I'm sure. (*He tucks the glove into his belt*)

HERACLES. Why are you doing that?

THESEUS. Why? Because she's gone. It'll have to wait.

HERACLES. Not at all. (*He indicates Hippolyte*) This one will do.

THESEUS. Oh, no, old boy, really. I mean, with the other I might have managed it, but . . .

HERACLES. Duty, my friend, duty. I'll leave you. (*He crosses to the steps* L)

THESEUS (*following Heracles*)   No, don't do that. Where are you going?

HERACLES (*going up the steps*)   To wash before lunch.

THESEUS. But—but—but you don't know where to go.

HERACLES. Someone will show me. Good luck! Be firm.

(HERACLES *exits to the palace.* THESEUS *looks at Hippolyte and smiles uncertainly*)

HIPPOLYTE. I gather you have some business with me?

THESEUS. Er—yes. Have you a few moments?

HIPPOLYTE. Well, I still haven't had my bath.

THESEUS. Do you always get up as late as this? (*He puts one foot on the upstage corner of the steps*)

HIPPOLYTE (*sitting on the bench*)   As a rule, much later. I have no energy whatever. Antiope's the lucky one: she's bursting with it. But I like nothing better than just to lie about. (*She lies back on the bench*)

THESEUS. I adore women who just lie about. (*He moves to Hippolyte and leans over her*) At home it is a dying art.

(THESEUS *beams at* HIPPOLYTE *who smiles in response. There is a pause*)

HIPPOLYTE (*at length*)   Yes; well?

THESEUS. Well?

HIPPOLYTE. What did you wish to say?

THESEUS. Oh. Oh, of course. (*He takes the glove from his belt but it does little to increase his confidence*) I hope you won't feel—whatever happens—I mean as far as I am concerned personally—that is to say, there *is* a distinction, isn't there?

HIPPOLYTE. I beg your pardon?

THESEUS. What I mean is, some things are personal while other things are—not.

HIPPOLYTE. Are they?

THESEUS. No, they aren't—other things, that is.

HIPPOLYTE. Oh.

THESEUS (*looking at the glove*)   This thing, for instance, is not. I do want you to understand that. (*He turns to her*) When you think of it, try to think of it like that.

HIPPOLYTE (*rising and crossing to the steps*)   I think I'll go and think of it in my bath.

THESEUS (*moving to R of her*)   No, no; you can't go yet. I mean, I haven't even done it.

HIPPOLYTE. Then do it while you're waiting for me.

THESEUS (*grasping her hand*)   Don't be silly: I can't do it alone. I only wanted to make everything clear beforehand.

HIPPOLYTE (*after a pause*)   You *are* trying to say *something*, I suppose?

THESEUS. Of course I am.

HIPPOLYTE (*crossing to the bench*) Perhaps you might be a little more coherent if you stopped fidgeting with that glove? (*She sits*)

THESEUS. But this is the whole point. You see, one obviously doesn't enjoy slapping people in the face, even with a glove. I mean—do you see what I mean?

HIPPOLYTE. Not quite.

THESEUS (*crossing and sitting* R *of Hippolyte on the bench*) Well, you mustn't think we're barbarians just because we're men. After all, there are men and men.

HIPPOLYTE. Which are you?

THESEUS (*rising*) Oh, do try and understand. Now, take this glove.

(HIPPOLYTE, *wondering, takes the glove*)

No, I meant, "take it for example." (*He takes the glove from her*) Now, if I strike you with it . . .

HIPPOLYTE. What!

THESEUS. I mean, *when* I strike you with it . . .

HIPPOLYTE. I shall be outraged.

THESEUS. Now, now, you mustn't be, that's the whole point: or rather you must be but only impersonally. I mean you mustn't take it out on me. It isn't really even my labour. I'm only doing all this as a friend. I assure you I am finding it hard enough. It wouldn't be with anyone but—don't you understand? I've dreamed about you every night since first we met.

HIPPOLYTE. We only met this morning.

THESEUS. That's right: then it must have started before we met. One doesn't want to be crude but—but I love you.

HIPPOLYTE. Of course you do.

THESEUS. Why "of course"?

HIPPOLYTE. Well, don't you love everyone?

THESEUS. Certainly not. I loathe most people.

HIPPOLYTE. You horrid little man!

THESEUS. Why horrid? Everybody loathes most people. If everybody loved everybody else, it would be a nice mix-up. It wouldn't be decent. Do you suppose I feel the same about that blacksmith creature that I feel about you? (*He crosses to the steps*)

HIPPOLYTE. Well, you certainly haven't attacked me yet as you did her, but I gather you are considering it.

THESEUS. But you I *have* to attack. I mean one must do what is right. Duty is duty, as someone said. What I want you to know is—the moment I saw you I wanted to protect you.

HIPPOLYTE. By clouting me with a glove.

THESEUS. No, that was a later idea. I wanted to gaze at you, to touch you, to stroke your hair, to . . .

HIPPOLYTE. Oh! Why didn't you say so? You mean you want to breed with me?

THESEUS (*moving down* L) Good Heavens, no! Really! I mean to say! What do you take me for?

HIPPOLYTE. Then in simple language—and please forgive my being so obtuse—what precisely *do* you want?

THESEUS (*kneeling*) I want—I want to serve you.

HIPPOLYTE. You mean you've come to see me about a job?

(HERACLES *and* ANTIOPE *enter from the palace and stand at the top of the steps*)

THESEUS (*almost weeping with frustration*) Oh, no! No! (*He rises*) Why can't you understand? (*He hurls the glove to the ground in violent despair, then notices Heracles and Antiope*) For the love of Ares, how long have *you* been listening?

HERACLES. A few moments.

ANTIOPE. Lunch is ready.

HIPPOLYTE. Oh, dear; and I still haven't had my bath.

HERACLES (*to Theseus*) How are you doing?

THESEUS. Of all the low disreputable tricks . . .

HERACLES. Were you firm?

THESEUS. We—we simply couldn't understand each other.

HERACLES. So I gathered. Perhaps I can help. (*He comes down the steps to* L *of Hippolyte*) When my friend appeared to be offering himself as your slave, he was speaking of the subjection of his heart.

THESEUS. Exactly.

HERACLES. In our world the subjection of a man's heart to a woman is a routine formula of chivalry. It helps to reconcile her to her subjection in other respects to him.

HIPPOLYTE (*rising*) I am sure I must sound terribly provincial but what exactly is chivalry?

HERACLES. A kind of game, madam. And like many games, taken too seriously, it tends to become an obsessive reality. The result is we men are often not quite as free as we boast—and women rather freer.

HIPPOLYTE. It sounds rather a nice game.

HERACLES. Madam, I think you have the makings of a dangerous woman: at least in our society.

ANTIOPE. Shall we go in to lunch?

(HERACLES *gives* ANTIOPE *his arm.* HIPPOLYTE *takes that of* THESEUS *and all four exit to the palace. The music of the lyre is heard and the lights fade with the exception of the spots on the niches* R *and* L. *The curtains in front of the niches rise, revealing* HERA *and* ZEUS)

HERA (*complacently*) Will you walk into my parlour said the spider to the fly?

ZEUS. Do you think that is what is happening?

HERA. Don't you?

ZEUS (*twinkling*) You may be right, my dear. We'll see. We'll see.

CURTAIN

ACT II

Scene i

Scene—*A courtyard inside the Palace. Two hours later.*

The courtyard or patio is used largely as an outdoor living-room, as is still customary in gentle climates, and is immediately inside the double doors seen in the previous Act, and which are now R with wide steps leading up to them. The reverse side of the watch-tower is above the doors, and set in it is a massive door with bolts and lock and a heavy iron grid across it. From the tower, a terrace with steps leads across and down L, so that the courtyard appears to be sunken. At the back of the terrace there is an outer containing-wall, three feet high, from which columns support the roof. Only the sky is visible beyond. At the left end of the terrace there is a curtained entrance to the inner rooms of the palace. A vine, with bunches of grapes, is growing on the upstage side of the tower and along the balustrade. There is a fountain and small pool C, with a foot-high marble surround. Creepers and flowering plants decorate the courtyard. Above the fountain there is a slightly curved low table, shaded by a large white umbrella. There are four chairs set above the table.

(See the Ground Plan at the end of the Play)

Before the CURTAIN *rises, the music of the lyre is heard in the darkness.*

When the CURTAIN *rises, the general lighting grows, illuminating the* FRONTCLOTH, *and spots are focused on the niches* R *and* L. HERA *and* ZEUS *are in their places.*

ZEUS. Observe; I am punctual. Shall we proceed?

HERA. I am not quite happy. You have unsettled me.

ZEUS. I, my dear?

HERA. That Antiope has a soft centre. These old-fashioned methods of hers are—out of date. I mistrust kid gloves.

ZEUS. Were you thinking by chance that the moment is approaching for you to intervene?

HERA. I didn't say so.

ZEUS. For my part I should have said Antiope was a doughty fighter: in her own rather specialized way. It could be that my boy has met his match. Still, I'll back him if you're in a betting mood. Two dolphins to a goat?

HERA. Hmm! Let's see what luncheon has done to them.

The music swells. The lights on the niches R *and* L *fade and the gauze curtains come down in each niche.*

When the FRONTCLOTH *rises, the two* QUEENS *and the two* HEROES *are sitting at the tail-end of lunch.* ANTIOPE *is seated above the left end*

32

of the table, HERACLES *is seated* L *of it,* HIPPOLYTE *above the right end and* THESEUS R *of it. The men's arms and armour are piled up* C *on the balustrade.* DIASTA *is perched on the balustrade up* RC, *clasping a wine-decanter and looking out to sea. The atmosphere is relaxed and urbane. The music continues softly under the dialogue.*

ANTIOPE. A final glass of wine, my lord?

HERACLES. No, thank you. I am far too contented already.

HIPPOLYTE (*to Theseus*) And you, my lord?

THESEUS. Well, thank you. It is excellent wine.

HIPPOLYTE. Diasta, some wine for my lord.

DIASTA (*rising leisurely*) Antiope, have you seen the fleet from here? It looks so pretty.

ANTIOPE. I saw it this morning.

DIASTA. Half the men are overboard, clinging to the side of the ships. What are they doing?

HIPPOLYTE. What are they doing, my lord?

HERACLES. Scraping the hull after the voyage, I expect.

DIASTA. May I go down and watch? You've finished luncheon.

ANTIOPE. If you like.

HIPPOLYTE. But leave us the wine.

DIASTA. Oh, yes. (*She puts the decanter on the table beside Theseus*) Help yourself, will you? Does anyone want the last peach?

ANTIOPE. I don't think so.

(DIASTA *takes a peach from the plate on the table and exits up the steps* R)

HERACLES (*amused*) Hm. How customs differ!

THESEUS. They do indeed.

ANTIOPE. What had you in mind particularly?

HERACLES. We keep our servants on a tighter rein.

HIPPOLYTE. What do you mean?

THESEUS (*taking some grapes from the plate*) Well, for one thing they wouldn't be allowed to slop about like that on duty. If they dared behave like that, we'd skin the hides off them. Not that I'm criticizing, mind you.

ANTIOPE. But they do their work.

THESEUS. I know, but the look of the thing. (*He drops grapes into his mouth*)

HIPPOLYTE (*to Heracles*) Does it shock you, too, my lord?

HERACLES. No, but I find it—unfamiliar. At home, for instance, they do not address us by our given names as though—— as though they were our cousins. Even the blacksmith does it here.

ANTIOPE. But very often they *are* our cousins.

HIPPOLYTE. The blacksmith is our aunt.

(*The music fades*)

THESEUS. Really, you people have a passion for mixing everything up. Whoever heard of a royal blacksmith? *Why?* I mean—
but *why?*

HIPPOLYTE. Why is she a blacksmith? Because she's good at it
and people enjoy doing what they are good at.

THESEUS. But dignity; there is such a thing as dignity.

ANTIOPE. I had not noticed that she lacked it. We always think
rather the contrary.

HERACLES. Does everybody choose the work that pleases
them? Did you two, for example, choose to be queens?

ANTIOPE. No, but we could have chosen not to be.

HERACLES. How does it work, two queens upon a single
throne?

HIPPOLYTE. With us it works extremely easily.

ANTIOPE. The throne is broad, the queens are not.

HIPPOLYTE. That is a way of saying that my sister is very
industrious and I am very lazy. She enjoys work: I enjoy pleasure.
That is why we have divided the State functions as we have.
There is never anything to do as far as foreign affairs are concerned. But home affairs, as you can imagine, are a full-time
job.

THESEUS. You mean people always popping in and out of gaol,
that kind of thing?

HIPPOLYTE. No, our people are not lawless.

HERACLES. Strange. Women at home are proverbially moral
anarchists, with no respect for law whatever.

ANTIOPE. Perhaps it is your laws they privately disrespect.
Perhaps in that way you have demoralized them. As queens we
are lucky, for the Amazons by nature are neither lawless nor
competitive.

HERACLES. The second is a curious defect. How can you have
prospered? Is competition not the catapult of human endeavour?

ANTIOPE. Do they still believe that in Greece?

HIPPOLYTE. We have found it so wasteful.

ANTIOPE. And it makes for so much bad blood.

THESEUS. But it is human nature.

HIPPOLYTE. It isn't ours.

HERACLES. Why not?

HIPPOLYTE (*after a pause; to Antiope*) Why isn't it?

ANTIOPE. Well, it is hard to say. Perhaps because maternity
gives us a vested interest in creation rather than destruction. We
hate to waste our pains. Perhaps because there is a long tradition
of good manners in our state. Since everybody respects everybody, everybody can respect herself—including blacksmiths and
cup-bearers. To us it seems that you two gentlemen, for example,
are constantly seeking through a remarkable display of heroism
to prove something that we here all take for granted.

HERACLES. Which is?

ANTIOPE (*shrugging a little*) That you are entitled to respect. We here never think of ourselves as anything else.

(THESEUS *yawns*)

HIPPOLYTE. The little one is bored.

ANTIOPE. So I noticed. But the big one wasn't or I would have stopped. (*To Theseus*) Forgive me, my lord.

THESEUS. No, really I wasn't bored in the least. I was most interested, but it's a curious thing, intelligent conversation always makes me sleepy.

ANTIOPE (*rising*) We have lingered a long time.

(HERACLES *and* THESEUS *rise*)

Your company has beguiled us. (*She moves down* L) Unfortunately, they are waiting for me at my office.

HIPPOLYTE (*rising*) And I must hurry off, too, or I shall miss my afternoon nap as well as my bath.

ANTIOPE. Make yourself at home.

HIPPOLYTE (*crossing to* L) Ask for anything you want.

HERACLES. Thank you.

(ANTIOPE *and* HIPPOLYTE *exit* L. THESEUS *takes a cushion from his chair, puts it on the steps* R *and stretches himself full-length on the ground with his head on the steps*)

THESEUS. Delightful people. A bit upside-down, but delightful people. Glorious weather. Excellent lunch. Those oysters were delicious.

HERACLES. Theseus.

THESEUS. What is it, old boy?

HERACLES. For two pins I'd lie down in the sun, as well.

THESEUS. Well, do, old fellow.

HERACLES. But we didn't come here for a siesta.

THESEUS. No, but it's not a bad idea.

HERACLES. It is a very bad idea. What are we going to do?

THESEUS. Do?

HERACLES. We have to do something. We cannot possibly sail back without that infernal belt. It may be a ridiculous errand, as Antiope obviously thinks, but we should be still more ridiculous if we went home without it.

THESEUS. Of course. That's out of the question. (*He pauses*) Did you notice the tilt of Hippolyte's nose?

HERACLES (*moving up* RC) To blazes with her nose! And Antiope's eyes, also, and their whole confounded system. Pull yourself together. Can't you see the war has started? And you look like becoming the first casualty.

THESEUS. I? I never felt better. At peace with all the world. This place has a pleasant effect on one, you know. It makes me feel somehow—creative.

HERACLES. You look it. What were you thinking of creating?

THESEUS. I don't know; I just feel I'd like to create. Perhaps if I had Hippolyte's co-operation . . .

HERACLES. I daresay. But at present you'll have to make do with mine.

THESEUS. I am devoted to you, dear chap; but it is hardly the same thing. Somehow you and I always seem to break more than we make.

HERACLES. Yes, I wish you wouldn't wander from the point. (*He sits on the edge of the fountain*) We have facts to face. I begin to get seriously worried. What are we going to *do*? Since they refuse to hand over the infernal belt and also refuse to fight for it, what are we going to *do*?

(THESEUS *scratches his head. In the silence* ZEUS *intervenes. The voices of the* GODS *are heard through the loud-speakers*)

ZEUS (*off*)   You might pinch it.

HERA (*off*)   Well, really! Who's intervening now?

ZEUS (*off*)   Sorry, it just slipped out. You are entitled to your turn.

HERACLES (*to Theseus*)   What did you say?

THESEUS. I didn't say anything.

HERACLES. You did.

THESEUS. Oh? What did I say?

HERACLES. You said we might pinch it.

THESEUS. I'll swear I did not, but it's not a bad notion.

HERACLES. Bad? (*He rises*) It's magnificent. After all, now I think of it, it is precisely the advice the oracle gave us before we sailed.

THESEUS. What was that?

HERACLES (*moving up* c)   Dear Zeus, is there nothing you can remember? Ever?

THESEUS. Well, I can't remember it for the simple reason that I never really understood it. Nor—may I remind you—did you. Give it me again.

HERACLES.

> "A prize set free from lock and key,
>   Shall violence assuage . . ."

Mm: I can't remember the rest.

(THESEUS *laughs*)

(*He takes a scroll from the breast of his tunic*) Here it is. (*He reads*)

> "A prize set free from lock and key,
>   Shall violence assuage,
>   Stone walls do not a prison make
>   Nor iron bars a cage."

THESEUS. It comes back to me.

HERACLES (*moving down* C) Clearly the significance lies in the first half. It can mean only one thing: we have to pick the lock.

THESEUS (*rising and sitting on the steps* R) Fine! Now at least we know where we are.

HERACLES. Yes.

THESEUS. You sound doubtful.

HERACLES. I don't much care for it.

THESEUS. You don't? Why not?

HERACLES. Well, is it—is it ethical?

THESEUS. Is that a Greek word?

HERACLES. Certainly. It means, is it—is it right?

THESEUS. Oh, I don't think I am really a judge. In any case, is that our business? After all, we're only supposed to be heroes.

HERACLES (*moving down* L) Precisely: not cracksmen nor footpads nor thugs.

THESEUS. Oh, come, you must not let a few words of Antiope's knock you sideways.

HERACLES. I am not concerned with Antiope's opinions. I wish I had never clapped eyes on her. I was merely wondering whether purloining somebody else's property may not conceivably verge upon—upon—the dishonest. That may be too strong a word but could you call it heroic, exactly?

THESEUS. It will save a very great deal of trouble.

HERACLES. I know. Nor do I wish to give myself moral airs, but—but—I mean, how will it look in print? After all, one doesn't want to go down to history as a petty-pilferer.

THESEUS (*rising and picking up the cushion*) You know, there is something queer about the atmosphere of this place. (*He moves to the table*) If we were up against the Trojans or the Thracians or the Oechalians, we shouldn't even be arguing. We'd be after the thing by now and no nonsense. (*He tosses the cushion on to the chair*)

HERACLES. Then you think it is all right?

THESEUS. *I* think so. It seems to me there is no reason on earth why we shouldn't proceed in a decent, orderly, straightforward manner and just sneak off with the belt.

HERACLES. Your choice of words is felicitious.

THESEUS. Then let us not argue any more: let us act.

HERACLES. Very well. Now, the next problem to decide is when.

THESEUS. Well, now, if you like.

HERACLES. Mm. (*He crosses below Theseus to* R) I should have thought it hardly the kind of thing one can do in broad daylight. On the other hand, it is hardly the kind of thing to do after our hostesses have innocently gone to bed.

THESEUS (*thoughtfully*) No. No. Especially since they haven't invited us to stay the night.

HERACLES (*moving up* R) Besides, the sooner we are out of this place the better. It begins to get on my nerves.

THESEUS. I know; it does make you a bit jumpy, doesn't it? You have the feeling all the time that these women are up to no good. You don't quite know what they have up their sleeve. Candidly, I don't trust them.

HERACLES. Very well, then. We'll do it now. Are you ready?

THESEUS. Yes.

HERACLES (*crossing to the exit* L) Come on, then: let's go.

THESEUS (*following Heracles*) Right, let's go.

HERACLES (*stopping and turning*) Wait a minute. Where are you going?

THESEUS. What?

HERACLES. I mean, where *is* the damned thing?

THESEUS. Oh. Mm, I see what you mean. Well, clearly the first step is to find out where it is kept; that's all. (*He sits on the fountain*)

HERACLES. And how?

THESEUS. Well—well—we shall have to ask somebody, I suppose.

HERACLES. Ask somebody. "Excuse me, madam: I am a stranger in these parts. I wonder if you would be kind enough to tell me where you keep your jewellery?"

THESEUS. All right, how do *you* propose to set about it?

HERACLES. We must pump somebody, not ask them. We must find somebody to give us the information without their knowing it.

HIPPOLYTE (*off* L; *calling*) Hippo! Hippo!

(HIPPOLYTE *enters* L. *She is completely enveloped in a large bath-towel, save for one arm and shoulder which are still glistening wet.*

ANTHEA *follows her on.* THESEUS *rises.* ANTHEA *remains on the steps* L)

(*She crosses to* LC) Excuse me, have either of you seen Hippobomene about?

HERACLES. Hippobomene?

HIPPOLYTE. Yes, you know; the blacksmith. I can't get a moment's peace today. Her daughter has started to have her baby and I know she would like Hippo to be there. Anthea, you'll have to run down to the town and fetch her. You're certain to find her either in her house or at the forge.

(ANTHEA *crosses above the table towards the steps* R)

HERACLES. Perhaps I can find her for you? It might save time if I went to the forge while the girl goes to the house.

HIPPOLYTE. Would you? How very kind.

ANTHEA. Which is her house? I have never been there.

Hippolyte. You can see it from here. Come. (*She goes on to the terrace*)

(Anthea *moves to Hippolyte*)

It has a red roof, do you see? The one behind the market . . .

Heracles (*leading Theseus down* R; *quietly*) I'll try and get something out of the blacksmith if I find her. Meanwhile, you do your best with Hippolyte.

Theseus. Leave it to me. I'll handle it.

(Anthea *exits up the steps* R)

Hippolyte (*moving down* C) The forge is at the bottom of the long drive to the left.

Heracles. I shall find it.

Hippolyte. I am most grateful. You can't miss it.

(Heracles *exits up the steps* R. Hippolyte *smiles at Theseus and turns to go*)

Theseus. Your Highness.

Hippolyte (*stopping and turning*) Yes?

Theseus. Might I have a word with you?

Hippolyte (*moving* C) Again?

Theseus. Of course, if it is an imposition . . .

Hippolyte (*doubtfully*) No. (*She sits on the fountain*) What is it about this time?

Theseus. Oh, nothing in particular. I thought we might have a chat.

Hippolyte. A chat.

Theseus. Yes.

Hippolyte. Well, you begin.

Theseus (*sitting* R *of Hippolyte on the fountain*) Well—er—well, let's see. (*He pauses for a moment, feeling for a gambit*) In Athens we often keep our things in chests.

Hippolyte. Do you?

Theseus. Yes. (*He pauses*) Where do you keep your things?

Hippolyte. In chests.

Theseus. Really? Extraordinary. Er—what kind of things?

Hippolyte. I don't quite understand.

Theseus. Well, to put it another way, perhaps I *should* say what kind of chests?

Hippolyte. Different kinds. And you?

Theseus. Yes, different kinds.

Hippolyte. Why do you ask?

Theseus. Oh, no reason. It was just—it was interesting at luncheon to—er—learn the different customs in our different countries. In Athens, for instance . . .

Hippolyte. Tell me about Athens.

THESEUS. Ah, Athens! You should go there. Great spot. Centre of the world. Has everything. Shops, games, amphitheatres, dances. *Very* gay. No-one ever goes to bed.

HIPPOLYTE. I shouldn't like that.

THESEUS. Well, you can if you wish, of course, but no-one ever wishes. Afraid of missing something.

HIPPOLYTE. I should be afraid of missing bed.

THESEUS. You may think so, but wait till you've seen the Acropolis by moonlight. Mind you, the building is all a bit new at present but when it has mellowed . . .

HIPPOLYTE. What else is there?

THESEUS. What else? Oh, everything. Shops, games, amphitheatres . . . And the women! The loveliest in the world. And the life they lead!

HIPPOLYTE. Really? Explain to me.

THESEUS. Well, we treat 'em very, very well, I promise you.

HIPPOLYTE. Do you? I had always heard you treated them very much as we treat men.

THESEUS. Good Heavens, no! Keep 'em in a farm?

HIPPOLYTE. It certainly seemed a little hard to believe. After all, though it *is* quite a natural condition for men, it wouldn't be for women, would it?

THESEUS. Dear lady, I can assure you we do not put 'em in sheds: we put 'em on pedestals. They are treated with respect and consideration, they are revered, they are cherished, they are competed for, they are served, they are complimented, they are admired, they are worshipped, they are idolized. We open the door for them when they leave a room. We bow and scrape and generally carry on like maniacs.

HIPPOLYTE. Do they like that?

THESEUS. Like it? They eat it. In fact, they expect it. And what they expect they invariably get—and usually a bit more for full measure. Their slightest wish is law. We feed them the choicest tidbits, we dress them up in silks and satins; and scent them; and hang jewels on them till they look like a bunch of blazing stalagmites. We write odes to them and fight for them and sing to them and make little jokes to them. They have nothing to do and not a care in the world. They are not expected to be able to do anything or to *know* anything or even to *talk* intelligently. Indeed, the more idiotic they choose to be the better we like 'em. In short, they are relieved of any and every burden that a man can carry for them. And we'd even carry the remaining one if we could.

HIPPOLYTE (*wistfully*) It does sound rather delicious.

THESEUS. Oh, you've no idea. (*He moves close to her*) You really must come and see for yourself.

HIPPOLYTE. It is very far away.

THESEUS. I might find wings for you.

(Heracles, *looking rather glum, enters* r. Theseus *moves away from Hippolyte*)

Heracles (*moving* rc)   She wasn't there. I'm sorry.

Hippolyte.   Then I am sure Anthea will have found her. (*She rises*)

(Theseus *rises*)

It was most kind of you to take the trouble. Your friend is a treasury of the most surprising traveller's tales. I wonder if they can be true. (*To Theseus*) You must tell me more.

Theseus.   I should be happy to.

Hippolyte.   But now I simply must get myself dressed or the day will be over.

(Hippolyte *exits* l. Theseus *follows her to the doorway*)

Heracles.   I drew a blank as you see. (*He moves to* r *of the fountain*) How did you get on?

Theseus (*looking raptly after Hippolyte*)   Fine. Fine!

Heracles.   You did? Excellent. Where is it? Where is it kept?

Theseus.   Where is what kept? (*He turns and steps towards Heracles*)

Heracles.   The belt, you blockhead!

Theseus.   Oh, bless my soul! The thing went clean out of my mind.

Heracles (*holding his bursting temples*)   Zeus, give me restraint! (*He turns away for fear of doing Theseus an injury and moves to the balustrade up* lc)

Theseus (*following Heracles*)   I'm very sorry, dear fellow, but one can't remember everything.

(Hippobomene *enters hurriedly* r. *She sees only Theseus and stops dead in her tracks, terrified at meeting once again and alone, the little lunatic who had attacked her out of a clear sky. Then just as suddenly, with eyes starting, she picks up her skirts and runs down* l. Heracles *blocks her path and* Theseus *moves down* r *behind Hippobomene*)

Heracles.   Please, don't be alarmed. The unfortunate circumstances of our first meeting shall not be repeated.

Hippobomene.   Thank you. I should *hope* not.

Heracles.   We did not know you were the Queens' aunt.

Hippobomene.   I don't see what that has to do with it, but still—(*she steps upstage*) just now you must excuse me.

Heracles.   We owe you an apology.

Hippobomene.   That is quite all right, my lord, but I am in a hurry. My daughter is having a baby. (*She steps downstage*)

Heracles (*still barring her way*)   I understand you do odd jobs around the palace?

Hippobomene.   Yes, my lord, but at the moment I am not on duty. (*She steps upstage*)

HERACLES (*barring her way*) It must be an interesting post.

HIPPOBOMENE. Very: but I am in a great . . .

HERACLES. I suppose you are in charge of the—the furnaces?

HIPPOBOMENE. Yes, my lord.

HERACLES. And the plumbing generally? (*He looks at Theseus*)

HIPPOBOMENE. Yes, my lord.

HERACLES. And, I imagine, all such things as—well, locks and bolts. You *are* a locksmith, I take it, as well as a blacksmith?

HIPPOBOMENE. Yes, I am, my lord; and now if you'll excuse me . . . (*She tries to pass Heracles*)

THESEUS. The locks, eh? You are in charge of the locks?

HIPPOBOMENE. There *are* no locks today in Themiscyra.

HERACLES. No locks?

THESEUS. There must be locks.

HIPPOBOMENE. There is nothing to lock up or rather there is nobody to lock it against. May I go now, please?

(HERACLES *stands aside.* HIPPOBOMENE *crosses to the entrance* L)

THESEUS. No locks? Good lord!

HIPPOBOMENE (*stopping and turning*) I'm sorry; none at all. Except, of course, that one—(*she points to the door in the tower*) in the Crown Tower.

(HIPPOBOMENE *exits* L. HERACLES *and* THESEUS *look at each other*)

THESEUS. Nice work, old fellow. (*He crosses below the fountain to* RC)

HERACLES (*crossing to the tower door*) It doesn't look easy, does it?

THESEUS. Shall we start?

HERACLES. I could wish it were in a rather more secluded situation. (*He moves up* C *and gets Theseus's sword*)

THESEUS. One of us can keep watch. Now is as good a time as any. As far as I can see, the entire nation seems to have its mind on nothing but the birth of this baby. They seem to think it more important than war and self-preservation.

HERACLES (*moving to the tower door*) They may connect it with self-preservation.

THESEUS. I don't understand you.

HERACLES (*smiling*) They are a primitive people. (*He tries with the sword to break the lock*) Keep an eye open. Tell me when anyone's coming.

(THESEUS *looks up the steps and off* R, *then crosses below the fountain and looks off* L)

THESEUS. Any luck?

HERACLES. No. I can't use leverage because this wretched grid is in the way.

THESEUS. Can you remove the grid?

HERACLES. I'll try. (*He puts the sword down, carefully tests the grid bars, then grasps two of them and exerts all his strength, grunting as he does so*)

THESEUS (*glancing off* L; *quietly*)   Look out.

(HERACLES *moves down* R *of Theseus.*

HIPPOBOMENE *enters* L, *a beaming grandmother with a bundle in her arms.*

ANTIOPE *follows her on. They are both cooing and jubilant*)

ANTIOPE. Hippolyte! Where's Hippolyte? (*She crosses to* C) She must hear the news. They told us she was here.

HERACLES. She was here.

THESEUS. She went off to finish dressing.

HERACLES. I see all's well. Congratulations.

HIPPOBOMENE ⎫ (*together*)   Thank you.
ANTIOPE ⎭

(HIPPOBOMENE *sits on the fountain.* ANTIOPE *stands* R *of her with one knee on the edge of the fountain and looks at the baby*)

THESEUS (*looking over Antiope's shoulder*)   Is it a boy or a girl?

ANTIOPE. A girl, of course. Hippo would hardly be grinning from ear to ear if it were not.

HIPPOBOMENE. Oh, the blessed relief of it!

THESEUS (*joining in the birthday spirit*)   Well, she'll have four nice little brothers to look after her.

ANTIOPE. I think, my lord, that is a joke in not quite the best possible taste. (*She turns to the baby*) Widgie, widgie, widgie!

THESEUS (*surprised*)   I'm sorry. I understood that four little boys had been born before her. Well, I mean—where are they?

ANTIOPE. They were drowned, of course. Widgie, widgie, widgie, widgie!

THESEUS (*turning to Heracles*)   Well, really!

(THALESTRIS *enters* L *and moves to* L *of Hippobomene*)

THALESTRIS. Antiope, it really is too vexing. I hate to complain at a time like this: but the father of this child is obviously a useful strain, strong enough even to counteract Melanippe's unfortunate tendencies. I had just given instructions that he was to be used extensively and now I find Melanippe hasn't the faintest idea who he was.

ANTIOPE. Oh, dear!

THALESTRIS. I hate regimentation but really we shall have to insist that the men at the farm are all properly labelled and numbered. And our girls *must* make a note of who they are mating with. If this were not such a happy occasion, I should really be quite cross with Melanippe. Come, my dear, you must bring the child back. It's time she were fed. I have sent the news to Hippolyte.

ANTIOPE. Good. Excuse me.

(HIPPOBOMENE *rises. She,* ANTIOPE *and* THALESTRIS *exit* L. *Alone again,* THESEUS *looks at Heracles*)

THESEUS. Makes your blood run cold, doesn't it?

(HERACLES *moves to the tower door and resumes work on the grid*)

(*He mutters indignantly*) Labels! Numbers! Sheds!

(HERACLES *gives a grunt of exertion*)

How's it coming? (*He looks off* R, *then off* L, *then off* R *again*)

HERACLES (*with a gasp*) It's—coming. (*He continues to wrestle with the grid and presently succeeds in detaching it altogether, a bent and tangled wreckage of wrought iron*)

(ANTIOPE *enters* L. *She does not immediately observe what Heracles is about.* HERACLES *kneels by the door.* THESEUS *masks him*)

ANTIOPE (*moving down* L) I forgot to ask you. My sister and I wondered whether after your long sea-voyage you wouldn't care to spend the night ashore? We can make you very comfortable.

THESEUS (*uneasily*) Oh. You are very kind, madam, but—well, unfortunately . . .

ANTIOPE (*seeing the mangled grid*) What are you doing?

HERACLES (*after a moment; firmly*) We were about to open this door. (*He takes the detached grid down* R)

ANTIOPE. But whatever for?

HERACLES. Because . . .

THESEUS (*interrupting*) We thought, while you were busy, we might explore the Crown Tower. There must be a lovely view up there.

ANTIOPE (*crossing to the tower door*) Yes, there is. But why didn't you use the key? (*She takes a large key from its hook high on the tower wall, where it has been hanging unnoticed*)

THESEUS. We didn't know where it was.

ANTIOPE. You could have asked.

HERACLES. We could have, if our purpose had been as my lord Theseus has stated it. But he is in error.

THESEUS. I say!

HERACLES. Our purpose was not to admire the view but to commandeer a trophy of the war which through no fault of ours did not take place.

THESEUS. Oh, beautifully put.

ANTIOPE. I begin to understand. The belt.

HERACLES. That explanation did not occur to you?

ANTIOPE. What made you suppose it is kept in the Crown Tower?

HERACLES. Firstly, because it is called the Crown Tower and

the belt, you tell me, is the Amazonian equivalent of crown jewels. Secondly, because we learned that this is the only lock and key in the kingdom.

ANTIOPE. Oh. I see. I fear you have been misled. (*She moves down* c *and turns to look up at the tower*)

(*The two men also look up*)

It is called the Crown Tower simply because its turret-top, as you may have noticed, resembles a crown. It is kept locked only for safety. Children used often to play in it and two years ago a little girl fell from the turret and was killed. That is why the key is hung beyond a child's reach. (*She replaces the key, then crosses between the men towards the exit* L)

HERACLES. You must forgive our mistake.

ANTIOPE. No, I think perhaps the apology is due from me. (*She stands* L *of the fountain*)

HERACLES. From you?

ANTIOPE. It is my obstinacy that seems to have reduced two celebrated heroes to the indignity of stealing.

HERACLES. I resent your language, madam.

THESEUS. So do I.

HERACLES. You withheld from us the honour of war. You could not expect to withhold from us, however, its proper spoils.

THESEUS. That's the line.

ANTIOPE. We have different phrases for the same thing.

HERACLES. I can understand your bitterness, madam.

ANTIOPE. Bitter? Oh, no. On the contrary I am a little intrigued. Stealing is such an old-fashioned, indeed, obsolete, practice here that I find it quaint.

THESEUS. Obsolete? Do you mean to tell me you don't even have thieves in this—this inhuman country of yours?

ANTIOPE. Oh, we did have them, of course, several generations ago, but we found them rather a nuisance so we had to get rid of them.

THESEUS. Really? How, pray? By drowning?

ANTIOPE. Oh, no. They were women.

THESEUS. How, then?

ANTIOPE. Oh, simply by making a special fuss of them generally. We had a home devoted to their use—far more luxurious than the palace. Anyone suffering from andritis was automatically admitted.

THESEUS. Andritis?

ANTIOPE. Yes, it was called that because—if you will forgive me—the patients obviously suffered from an almost masculine sense of inferiority. The logical cure was to make them feel favoured rather than looked down upon. That was what the home was for.

HERACLES (*pacing up and down stage; suddenly blazing*) I find this conversation unbearable. Doubtless I was meant to. But we are not patients, thieves, kleptomaniacs or moral degenerates. We are men charged with a mission. It is our duty to acquire a certain belt, just as it is your duty to prevent us. And I see no need for recrimination on either side. Naturally, I understand your resentment at finding your property wantonly damaged by visitors enjoying your hospitality; but how were we to know the belt is not kept there?

ANTIOPE. Why didn't you ask?

THESEUS. Ask where it is kept?

ANTIOPE. It seems the simplest way, doesn't it?

HERACLES. Well—well, where *is* it kept?

ANTIOPE. Oh, by a long tradition, it is always kept in the queen's bedchamber. I must send Hippobomene·to remove the debris. (*She moves to the exit* L, *but turns abruptly*) You did say you would stay the night, didn't you?

(THESEUS *looks to Heracles for a lead.* HERACLES *moves away and for a moment is silent. Presently he turns and faces Antiope*)

HERACLES. Thank you, madam. We shall be delighted.

ANTIOPE. I am so glad. Diasta will show you your rooms.

(ANTIOPE *exits* L. THESEUS *turns slowly, stares at Heracles, and sits very deliberately on the fountain*)

THESEUS. Whew! You certainly fall on your feet. I wish to Zeus *I* were a son of Zeus.

(*The lights dim to* BLACK-OUT. *The* FRONTCLOTH *falls and the curtains at the niches* R *and* L *rise. Spots come up on the niches where* ZEUS *and* HERA *are in their places*)

ZEUS. It unfolds, it unfolds. Do you like the story?

HERA. I do not like the way it points at present. That son of yours was born too lucky. Antiope must be mad. She is a disgrace to her sex. To give in without a struggle!

ZEUS. Be fair, my dear: she has struggled. How, pray—in her shoes—would *you* have tackled the invader?

HERA. Can you not guess?

ZEUS. I think I can, but tell me.

HERA. I would have sent him packing with a flea in his ear. Courtesy and tolerance are wasted on such ruffians. He should have met a woman that *was* a woman.

ZEUS. That was a woman. You mean an ex-woman.

HERA. You know what I mean. I would have given him a taste of his own medicine.

ZEUS. Yes, that would have been interesting to watch. Why don't you prompt her, just a little?

HERA. Perhaps I shall, since you suggest it.

ZEUS. Well, it *is* your turn.

HERA. I know, I know.

ZEUS. A taste of his own medicine. I know a fable with that
title. May I tell it to you?

HERA. I expect I have heard it.

ZEUS. No, for I have only just invented it. Once upon a time
there lived in a forest glade two friends. One was a beautiful
giraffe of great wisdom, with a most graceful neck, the other was
a small monkey of great cunning, with a heliotrope rump. Now,
owing to the length of her beautiful neck, the giraffe was able to
eat all the choicest leaves and fruit high up in the trees, so that
the monkey after an arduous climb found all the best branches
bare. One day he resolved no longer to rest content merely with
whatever leaves were left over for him. So the cunning little
monkey addressed the wise and beautiful giraffe as follows. "Oh,
dear giraffe, how long are you going to put up with it?" "Put up
with what?" said the giraffe. "The life you lead," said the
monkey. "Surely you carry patience too far? Why should *you* not
be allowed to climb up trees and swing on branches as I do? Are
you an inferior animal? No! Then why should you not share my
rights? Are you a less intelligent animal? No! Then why should
you be confined to the ground and forbidden to skip among the
tree-tops? Why should you be treated as a second-class beast?
When will you emancipate yourself?" Hearing these words, the
giraffe became uneasy. Whereas before she was wont to count her
blessings, now she began to count her grievances. Then one
morning she unfurled a flag of defiance and, crying "To the
barricades," began to climb a tree. But she had not proceeded
far before she fell; and, in doing so, nearly broke her beautiful
neck. In fact it was permanently dislocated and the tragedy was
she was never able to reach to her full height again. Thus cunning corrupted wisdom, the monkey obtained complete command
of the tree and the beautiful giraffe had ever after to rest content
with whatever leaves were left over for her.

HERA. Is that all?

ZEUS. Yes. Do you like it? I thought of giving it to Aesop to
polish.

HERA. Has it a moral?

ZEUS. Oh, only that giraffes are none the better for a dislocated neck.

HERA. It is a silly story. I don't understand it.

ZEUS. If I had expected you to, I should not have told it.
There is too much monkey in me for that.

HERA. Don't you think one story at a time is enough?

ZEUS. Certainly, my dear.

(*A morning light spreads over the scene*)

Am I holding things up?

The lights on the niches R *and* L *fade and the gauze curtains come
down in each niche.*

Scene 2

SCENE—*The same. The next morning.*

When the FRONTCLOTH *rises, the table, umbrella, chairs and grid, along with the Heroes' arms and armour, have been removed.* HERACLES *is seated on the right side of the fountain, looking off* R. ZEUS *is heard speaking through the loudspeaker.*

ZEUS (*off*) Yes, it is morning. (*He calls*) Diasta! Bring the boy his breakfast.

(DIASTA *enters* L. *She carries a tray with a bowl of fruit and some wine, which she puts on the down-stage side of the fountain*)

DIASTA. Do you like fish or eggs for breakfast?

(HERACLES *does not answer*)

Hi! Do you like fish or eggs for breakfast?
HERACLES. What? No, thank you.

(DIASTA *exits* L. HERACLES *stares at the fruit for a moment without concentration, takes a bunch of grapes, washes them in the fountain, then rises and strolls moodily with them to the steps* R.
ANTIOPE *enters* L *and watches Heracles in silence for a few moments*)

ANTIOPE. Good morning, my lord. (*She moves* LC)
HERACLES (*turning*) Good morning.
ANTIOPE (*after a moment*) Is your friend up?
HERACLES (*moving to the fountain*) I haven't seen him. It is early.
ANTIOPE. No, the sun is quite high.
HERACLES. Then it is late. (*He replaces the bunch of grapes on the tray*)

(ANTIOPE *regards Heracles ruefully*)

ANTIOPE. Do not be sad, my lord.
HERACLES. I have not your gift for gaiety. Nor your cause for it.
ANTIOPE. I am not gay, my lord.
HERACLES (*turning abruptly up* C) How's the new baby?
ANTIOPE (*after a pause*) Well.
HERACLES. And the mother?
ANTIOPE. I have just come from her bedside. She is sleeping rosily.
HERACLES. She sleeps in triumph. She is to be envied.
ANTIOPE. Did you not sleep, my lord?
HERACLES. Too well, I thank you.
ANTIOPE. You are more fortunate than I. I lay awake all night.
HERACLES (*looking at her*) Were you expecting me?

ANTIOPE. There were no guards, no arms, no locks, no bolts, no sentinels. You could have taken the belt—and me; both of which I think you wanted. Yet I was not expecting you.

HERACLES. You know me, madam.

ANTIOPE. Yes. And it is a high honour, my lord.

HERACLES (*moving down* R) I am glad you honour me, for I do not honour myself. I am a fool, madam. I should have come.

ANTIOPE. What held you?

HERACLES. My folly. I cannot even blame my ancient enemy.

ANTIOPE. Your enemy?

HERACLES (*crossing to her*) The goddess Hera. She is prone to bedevil the work I do but this time a mortal magic was enough.

ANTIOPE (*moving up* L) It is not I that has bewitched you. It is Themiscyra.

HERACLES. Themiscyra or you. The result's the same. (*He turns and crosses to* R)

(THESEUS, *cheerful and shining, enters* L, *rubbing his hands expectantly. He sees Heracles first and crosses to him*)

THESEUS. Well, how did you get on, old boy? Where is it? Where's the booty? Where's the swag?

(HERACLES *indicates Antiope up* L *by looking at her*)

(*He turns and sees Antiope*) Oh, excuse me. I didn't see you.

ANTIOPE (*moving to* L *of the fountain*) What is there to excuse?

THESEUS (*moving to her*) Well, I couldn't have asked in front of you. I mean, one doesn't want to rub it in.

ANTIOPE. You are very delicate.

THESEUS. Well, one isn't a rhinoceros, you know. But let me give you one consolation: to lose to Heracles is no disgrace. In a way it's losing to Zeus himself; so what can you expect?

HERACLES. Theseus.

THESEUS. Yes, old fellow?

HERACLES. Your—er—condolences are misplaced.

THESEUS (*crossing to Heracles*) What do you mean?

HERACLES. I am not—that is, I haven't been—er—as completely successful as you assume.

THESEUS. I don't understand.

HERACLES. I have not achieved—the belt.

THESEUS. What? Why not?

HERACLES. Because—because—well, I haven't.

THESEUS. But whatever happened?

HERACLES. Nothing happened.

THESEUS. Nothing? Why not?

HERACLES. I am sorry. I failed you. I am sorry.

THESEUS. Do you mean there was some trick?

HERACLES. No—yes—in a sense, perhaps. But not really.

THESEUS. I simply do not understand.

ANTIOPE (*crossing to* R *of the fountain*) Let me explain. Your friend failed to remove the belt for a very simple reason.

THESEUS. What was that?

ANTIOPE. Because it was not there.

THESEUS. You mean—you tricked him?

ANTIOPE. No; he has another enemy more powerful than those he chooses for himself: the goddess Hera.

THESEUS. What has she to do with it?

ANTIOPE. The belt has disappeared. I suspect that she forestalled him. (*She sits on the fountain*)

THESEUS. Hera again! Well, of all the dirty tricks. It makes my blood boil. Why can't she leave you alone? It's a shame. (*He crosses up* C) Talk about vindictive! (*He crosses down* R) Just because you're a bastard—that is, old fellow, just because Zeus every so often . . . And, after all, who wouldn't if one were Zeus? Unique opportunities, I mean—well, obviously. Well, there it is. Anyhow, even if you didn't get the belt, did you get . . .? No, no, it wouldn't be gentlemanly for you to tell me. What do we do next?

HERACLES. There is only one thing to do.

THESEUS. Yes?

HERACLES. We must return for further consultation with the oracle.

THESEUS. It's the devil of a long way.

HERACLES. A few weeks.

THESEUS. Besides, even if we do get another tip, why do you suppose we shall understand it any better than the last one?

HERACLES. Have you any alternative to suggest?

THESEUS. No. No, I don't think I have.

HERACLES. Nor have I. So let us waste no more time. Go down to the harbour like a good fellow and tell the men we're sailing immediately.

THESEUS (*turning to go*) I'll run and say good-bye to—to her sister.

HERACLES (*restraining Theseus*) We have no time. The tide's with us. We'll barely catch it.

THESEUS. But I shan't be a minute.

ANTIOPE. I *think* she's in her bath.

THESEUS. Not again!

HERACLES. I'll collect my chattels and join you. (*He pats Theseus on the shoulder and moves up* R)

THESEUS. Oh, dear. Well, good-bye, your highness.

(ANTIOPE *rises*)

Thank you for your hospitality. Please apologize for me to what's-her-name and give her my very kind regards. Tell her I'll be back soon. I'll look forward to it. (*He goes up the steps* R)

ANTIOPE. That will be nice. You may rely on a suitable welcome.

Theseus. Good. Charming of you. Good-bye.

(Theseus *exits* r. *There is a little silence*)

Heracles (*moving down* r *of Antiope*) I shall not see you again.

Antiope. That depends on what instructions you elicit from the oracle.

Heracles. We are not visiting the oracle. I told Theseus that we were, in order—in order to postpone argument. But we shall not return to molest you.

Antiope. Oh, my lord!

Heracles. We have troubled this strange place enough.

Antiope. But how can you return home empty-handed? What will you tell them?

Heracles. I shall tell them the truth; that you defeated me.

Antiope. It is a hateful phrase.

Heracles. You should find joy in it.

Antiope. You know I cannot.

Heracles. I can a little.

Antiope. But when you return? Can you face so much humiliation?

Heracles. My courage is not all in my arms. I must be as fearless as you have been.

Antiope. I? If you knew how I have been quaking since you came.

Heracles. I think you are quaking a little still.

Antiope. It is for another reason, my lord.

Heracles. I know. (*He takes her in his arms and kisses her at length*)

Antiope (*when her lips are freed*) I have visited Synope more than once. But this—has overtones.

Heracles. It is romance.

Antiope. It frightens me. It makes me not myself. Can that be good?

Heracles. It would depend on who your self may be. With you perhaps it is not good. Your self needs no revision. (*He kisses her*)

(Hippolyte *enters* l. *She is very sleepy and again in her négligé. She sees the embrace and moves to* l *of the fountain*)

Hippolyte (*blinking herself into wakefulness*) Well, for pity's sake, is this a farm? What *are* you doing?

Antiope (*smiling*) It is a little overspill.

Heracles. I will fetch my things.

(Heracles *exits* l. Hippolyte *watches him off then turns to* Antiope)

Hippolyte. What's happening?

Antiope. They are going.

HIPPOLYTE. Going? Going back? (*She moves above the fountain*) Do you mean they have given in?

ANTIOPE. Yes.

HIPPOLYTE. Oh, darling, this is wonderful. But what a struggle it has been. Aren't you happy? Why do you look so glum?

ANTIOPE. I am happy, yes. It is a welcome relief. I am happy: and I am unhappy. For Heracles is leaving. I shall not see him ever again.

HIPPOLYTE. But, dearest, that is what we wanted.

ANTIOPE. And now, in one sense, I want it more than ever. For now there's no fight in me. If he had stayed, we should have lost—everything.

HIPPOLYTE. Darling!

(HERACLES *enters* L *wearing his armour, lion-skin and arms.* HIPPOLYTE *withdraws discreetly to the terrace*)

HERACLES (*facing Antiope*) Good-bye.

ANTIOPE. Good-bye, my lord.

HERACLES (*crossing to her*) I shall remember you.

ANTIOPE. We will remember each other.

(*Sailors' voices are heard in the distance calling "Anchors aweigh"*)

HIPPOLYTE (*with a sudden cry*) Antiope! They've sailed.

HERACLES (*moving quickly to* R *of Hippolyte*) What!

HIPPOLYTE. They have weighed anchor and are sailing. Look!

HERACLES (*looking off*) By Zeus, the little toad's forgotten me. Theseus! (*He puts his hands to his mouth and bellows*) Ahoy! Ahoy! Oi! Ahoy!

(HERACLES *dashes off* R *as fast as his legs can carry him*)

(*Off; calling*) Oi! Oi! Ahoy!

HIPPOLYTE. He'll never catch them. He hasn't a chance. They've a following wind.

ANTIOPE (*her eyes closed in foreboding*) Oh, merciful heavens! He will be back . . .

CURTAIN

ACT III

Scene i

Scene—*The same. A few minutes later.*

When the Curtain *rises, the full stage is in view, the gauze curtains on the niches* r *and* l *are up, the spots are focused on them and though* Hera *is in her place* Zeus *is not.* Hippolyte *and* Antiope, *in attitudes of arrested movement, are craning over the balustrade up* c, *watching in despair as the ships move out. They remain still as statues throughout the following dialogue between the Gods.* Hera *waits patiently a few moments until* Zeus *arrives.*

Hera. Where have *you* been? The bar?

Zeus. Well, I did happen to run into Dionysus, my dear. Hadn't seen him for centuries. Am I late?

Hera (*jerking her head towards the Queens*) They're waiting for you.

Zeus. Ah, yes. Those poor girls. I fear it's looking rather badly for your side. Why don't you take a hand? I'm sure you're itching to. The results might be—quite unexpected.

Hera (*suspiciously*) What do you mean by "unexpected"?

Zeus. Perhaps it was the wrong word. Let us say "instructive".

Hera. If I *do* intervene, your boy will lose: I promise you.

Zeus. Perhaps, perhaps. Shall we proceed?

(*The two* Queens *snap into mobility, wailing after the departing fleet.* Heracles' *voice is heard faintly in the distance*)

Antiope. They're too far out by now. They haven't seen him. Oh, *dear*, why haven't they seen him?

Hippolyte. Why haven't they heard him? He's bawling and screaming his head off—dancing up and down like mad.

Antiope. They haven't seen him.

Hippolyte. My word, isn't he in a rage! He's tearing up whole trees by the roots.

Antiope. Too late. They're rounding the headland.

Hippolyte (*turning to Antiope*) Look at him. He's tearing up the bollards on the quay. Mercy, he'll wreck the harbour.

Antiope. They haven't seen him. They've gone. He mustn't come back here. (*She moves down* l)

(Hippolyte *follows to* r *of Antiope*)

What shall I do? What shall I do?

Hippolyte. There, darling, there. They'll turn back soon. Somebody will remember him. Come now, don't be upset.

53

ANTIOPE (*kneeling by the fountain*) Oh, Ashtoreth, dear goddess of Heaven, protect me. Have pity on me. Oh, Ashtoreth, help me. (*She weeps*)

HERA. Ashtoreth! A great help that foreign impostor will be.

ZEUS (*mildly*) Oh, she has her following.

HIPPOLYTE. Darling, don't cry.

ANTIOPE. I am afraid. How can I trust myself? (*Suddenly*) Hippolyte, I have an idea.

HIPPOLYTE. What is it?

ANTIOPE. Do you think it would be very wrong—I mean, do you think Ashtoreth would mind if, just for this once, we tried another goddess?

HIPPOLYTE (*doubtfully*) Well—I don't really know. She mightn't. Why?

ANTIOPE. I was thinking of Hera.

HIPPOLYTE. Hera?

ANTIOPE. You see, we do know she has always resented Heracles' very existence. He told me so. I just thought she might be quite glad of the opportunity to put a spoke in his wheel.

HIPPOLYTE. But what could she do?

ANTIOPE. I don't know. She might think of something. She might make Theseus remember and turn back.

HIPPOLYTE. I suppose it's just worth trying. After all, Ashtoreth has never been the jealous type; a little inattentive, sometimes, but never petty.

ANTIOPE. Exactly. Let us try. (*She kneels up*) Hera! Dear Hera, forgive this importunity from a complete stranger, but please, please, would it be a great nuisance to you to put a little sense into Theseus' fat head and send him back here immediately?

(*There is a silence.* HIPPOLYTE *runs to the balustrade and looks over*)

ZEUS (*to Hera*) I think someone is talking to you, my dear.

HERA. I heard, thank you.

ANTIOPE. Anything happening?

HIPPOLYTE. Not a thing. Sailing straight on. I can just see the last ship. Try again.

ANTIOPE (*desperately*) Hera! Hera, are you *listening*? I am desperate. If Heracles comes back, he will triumph. He doesn't know it but I do. I've no resistance left. Won't you, *won't* you kindly oblige me? Is there any little offering you would care for in return? A sheep? An ox? A couple of male babies? You see, I don't quite know what your tastes are but we *mustn't* lose the belt and I am sure you'd hate that big bruiser to get it. Wouldn't you? (*To Hippolyte. After a pause*) Anything?

HIPPOLYTE. No, nothing.

ANTIOPE. Oh, dear!

HIPPOLYTE (*moving to Antiope*) Now, now; let's not start

panicking again. That isn't like you. You will have to be strong, that's all. Make him think he bores you.

Antiope (*rising and moving up* L) It's a little late for that.

Hippolyte (*looking off* R) He's coming. Compose yourself.

(Heracles *enters* R, *his face glistening with rage and with sweat from his exertions*)

Heracles. The toad! The little toad! The addle-headed toad! May Zeus and all the merciful gods torment him for ever and ever. May he be shackled alive in the flames and smoke of hell for ever and ever. May he suffocate for a million days in darkness. (*He moves down* R)

Hippolyte (*crossing to Heracles*) Are you referring to your little friend?

(Antiope *goes to the balustrade*)

Heracles. Friend? Would a friend desert me in an hour of crisis?

Hippolyte. He has not done it on purpose. We are all a little forgetful sometimes.

Heracles (*crossing feverishly below the fountain to* L) Sometimes!

Hippolyte. Come now, don't be upset. Someone is bound to remember you soon. I was just saying so to Antiope. After all, you are not exactly the kind of trifle that one can overlook. They'll be turning back soon. You'll see.

Antiope (*suddenly*) Look! They're turning.

(Hippolyte *rushes to Antiope.* Heracles *moves up* L *of the Queens*)

Hippolyte. They are, they are.

(*The mortals freeze, following the fleet out at sea*)

Hera. Well, now: fancy that. Somehow I thought they might.

Zeus. Yes, my dear. So did I.

Antiope (*to the skies; heartfelt*) Oh, thank you, thank you.

Heracles. Praise be to Zeus!

Hera. To Zeus, indeed! Well, really! Did you hear that?

(Zeus *puffs out his cheeks and blows*)

Zeus. Yes, my dear. (*He blows again*)

(*A low rumble of thunder is heard, followed by the sound of a rising wind*)

Hera. What are you doing? What was that?

Zeus. Nothing, my dear; a little flatulence, that's all.

(Zeus *blows a third time, now more forcibly. Indeed it is an almost lewd-sounding exhalation that merges into a roll of thunder.* Hera *begins to look suspicious. The sky darkens. The thunder, interspersed with lightning, mounts*)

HIPPOLYTE (*pointing over the balustrade*) Look!

HERACLES. My god, look at them! What's happening? They will be wrecked. Their sails are flapping helplessly. How can they live in this? They'll sink. No, look! They're being borne back by the gale, stern foremost. Like corks in a giant unseen hand. They're headed westward for the Bosphorus.

ANTIOPE. Oh, no! They can't! They mustn't!

HERA (*to Zeus*) You son of a Titan!

ZEUS. Who—me?

HERACLES (*shouting against the storm*) Come back, come back!

(HERACLES *runs off* R)

(*Off; shouting*) Come back!

HIPPOLYTE (*running to the steps* R *and calling*) Don't be so silly! How can they even hear you? Hey! My lord!

(*There is a flash of forked lightning and a crash of thunder. A beam of light catches* HIPPOLYTE *who stands transfixed* RC. HERA'S *voice is heard through the loud-speakers*)

HERA. Hippolyte.

(*The wind fades and the thunder dies away*)

HIPPOLYTE (*turning*) Who was that?

HERA (*through the loud-speakers*) Come here.

HIPPOLYTE. Who's talking to me?

ZEUS (*to Hera; smugly*) I see you are about to take a hand.

HERA. You challenged me to do so.

ZEUS. I'm not complaining. What are you going to do?

HERA. This daintiness down there has gone on long enough. Remember Amphytrion? The gentleman whose body you— requisitioned?

ZEUS. Well—borrowed for a while. Yes?

HERA. An interesting precedent. I hope I shall entertain you. (*Through the loud-speakers*) Hippolyte, go to sleep.

HIPPOLYTE (*puzzled*) I shall not go to sleep.

HERA (*through the loud-speakers*) Hippolyte, I said "Go to sleep".

HIPPOLYTE. Go to sleep yourself, whoever you are.

HERA (*through the loud-speakers*) Lie down, Hippolyte. Lie down by the fountain.

HIPPOLYTE. Whatever for?

HERA (*through the loud-speakers*) Do you begin to feel sleepy?

HIPPOLYTE. I always feel sleepy.

HERA (*through the loud-speakers*) Do you feel sleepier than usual?

Hippolyte. No, I don't.

Hera (*through the loud-speakers*) Then try to. Lie down and have a nice little nap.

Hippolyte. I shall do neither the one nor the other.

Hera (*through the loud-speakers*) Oh, yes, you will.

(*There is a flash of lightning, rather more pink in tone than those which have preceded it, and then a peal of thunder.* Hippolyte *falls to the ground, apparently insensible.* Antiope *rushes to Hippolyte.*

Hera *disappears from her niche. The general lighting returns to normal daylight*)

Antiope (*kneeling beside Hippolyte*) Darling, what is it? What's happened? Was it the lightning? Were you struck? Hippolyte, answer me.

Zeus (*to Hera*) I didn't do that. Did you? (*He looks across and sees she has gone*)

(Hera's *voice is heard through the loud-speakers*)

Hera (*off*) Remember Amphytrion—Amphytrion—Amphytrion . . .

Hippolyte (*her eyes still closed*) Amphytrion . . .

Antiope. What? Hippolyte, Hippolyte. (*She slaps Hippolyte's hands*) Oh, darling, answer me.

(Hippolyte *opens her eyes and sits up briskly. The gauze curtains come down over the niches* R *and* L *and the spots on them fade*)

Hippolyte. Well, that was quick. (*She puts her hand to her head*) Mm, a slight dizziness, perhaps, but that's not surprising.

Antiope (*rising*) Hippolyte, are you all right?

Hippolyte. Of course I'm all right. (*She gets to her feet, rejecting Antiope's helping hand*) Don't fuss me. Time is short. I've work to do: a great deal of work.

Antiope. Work? Darling, are you sure you're all right?

Hippolyte (*thundering*) Of course I'm all right. Now then. Let me see. (*She crosses below the fountain and stands up* L) First of all, I shall need more staff.

Antiope. Staff?

Hippolyte. More staff at my Ministry.

Antiope. What do you mean by *more* staff? You haven't any at present.

Hippolyte (*moving to the entrance* L) Haven't I? Then it's time I had.

Antiope. Yes, dear. And what will you do with it?

Hippolyte. What do you think, woman? (*She claps her hands and calls*) Diasta! (*She moves down* C)

Antiope (*humouring her*) Darling, do something for me. You go and lie down and take a nice little nap. (*She moves up* R *of the fountain*)

(DIASTA *enters* L, *munching a peach*)

DIASTA (*moving* LC) Did you call, Hippolyte?

HIPPOLYTE (*turning furiously on Diasta*) Don't call me Hippolyte, girl! How dare you? I am your Queen. And curtsy when you appear before me.

DIASTA. What? What for?

HIPPOLYTE. There's not enough discipline in this place. It's preposterous! No-one's *afraid* of anyone. There are going to be some changes round here. Stand up, girl: don't slouch. Can you write?

DIASTA (*bewildered*) No.

HIPPOLYTE. "No, your highness."

DIASTA. No, your highness.

HIPPOLYTE. Then send me somebody who can. Oh, and find Thalestris for me. (*She crosses to the tower and examines the lock and bolts on the door*)

(DIASTA *turns to* ANTIOPE *for confirmation and, to her surprise, receives it. She runs off* L, *rather frightened*)

Antiope, we must proclaim an immediate state of emergency.

ANTIOPE. Of course we must, darling. Why didn't I think of that before?

HIPPOLYTE. We must put the entire country on a war footing.

ANTIOPE. Yes, darling, we'll put it there after you've had a nice little nap.

HIPPOLYTE. You've got naps on the brain. Is that the way to conduct a war?

ANTIOPE. Well, I wouldn't know, but don't you think we should be wiser to stick to the constitution? You continue to look after your department and I continue to look after mine.

HIPPOLYTE. During the emergency, everything *is* in my department. My department is the department of war. (*She indicates the bolt*) This seems a bit rusty. Is it sound?

ANTIOPE. Yes, dear, I think so. Does it matter?

HIPPOLYTE. Certainly it matters. We're going to need it.

ANTIOPE. Are we? What on earth for?

HIPPOLYTE. For our first prisoner of war: for Heracles—if I have any trouble with him, as I certainly shall. Heaven knows, I've had enough with his father.

ANTIOPE. What? Hippolyte, listen to me. To be struck by lightning is a *very* nasty thing. If you go to bed and have a nice little nap . . .

HIPPOLYTE. It will save time if *you* listen to me, woman. You sent for me and now that I am here I expect your obedient co-operation.

ANTIOPE. I sent for you? What *are* you talking about?

HIPPOLYTE. Not five minutes ago you prayed to me on your

bended knees to come down and help you. Very well, I have come.

ANTIOPE (*stepping back; appalled*) Hera!

HIPPOLYTE. You're not very quick, are you?

ANTIOPE. But where's Hippolyte?

HIPPOLYTE. She's having a little nap. That's what you've been clamouring for, isn't it?

ANTIOPE. But where *is* she? Is she—in there with you?

HIPPOLYTE. Don't be silly, girl. There's barely room for *me* in here.

ANTIOPE. But is she *all right*? Will you promise?

HIPPOLYTE. Of course, of course. I've come to help you, haven't I?

ANTIOPE. But—but how? Have you a plan?

HIPPOLYTE. Certainly. The Amazons will fight!

ANTIOPE. What? Oh, no!

HIPPOLYTE. No? You wait and see.

ANTIOPE. But I prayed for you to *help* us.

HIPPOLYTE. That's right: I'm helping you.

ANTIOPE. Help us? You'll get us slaughtered.

HIPPOLYTE. Nonsense! We outnumber them by ten to one.

ANTIOPE. But even if we win we shall have lost. Go back—go back to wherever you've come from and let us handle this in our own way, please. We weren't doing badly.

HIPPOLYTE. Weren't you! It seemed to me you were on the brink of defeat.

ANTIOPE. I won't allow it! I'll tell the Amazons who you are.

HIPPOLYTE. I shouldn't. If you do, I'll have no mercy on Themyscyra—nor on your sister.

ANTIOPE. Oh, no. You couldn't.

HIPPOLYTE (*wiggling her shoulders*) This shoulder is a little uncomfortable. I didn't know she had a touch of rheumatism.

ANTIOPE (*viciously*) Rheumatism! You wait till she gets her indigestion.

(HERACLES *enters dejectedly* R)

HERACLES. The storm's abated but there's not a sign of them.

HIPPOLYTE (*about to enjoy herself*) Ah, there he is. Our little problem child.

HERACLES. I beg your pardon?

ANTIOPE. Please, take no notice, my lord. She wasn't talking to you.

HIPPOLYTE (*cheerfully*) Oh, yes, I was. My lord Heracles, I was speaking to your father a little while ago . . .

HERACLES. What!

HIPPOLYTE. He didn't say it in so many words but I *think* he'd like you to depart from here.

HERACLES. Is she out of her mind?

ANTIOPE. Well, in a sense . . .

HIPPOLYTE. Your father, who has an unusually affectionate nature, is even fond of you. He'd hate you to get hurt. That's why you're leaving.

HERACLES. Oh? So I'm leaving?

HIPPOLYTE. I think so. Isn't he, Antiope?

ANTIOPE. Well, we *are* a little crowded just now.

HIPPOLYTE. And we have some rather important business before us. To be blunt, you might be in our way.

HERACLES (*taking a menacing step forward*) I begin to think that you might be in mine.

HIPPOLYTE. We have been pretty tolerant of you so far. You arrived here without invitation and within five minutes you had over-stayed your welcome.

ANTIOPE. Oh, no!

HIPPOLYTE. Silence!

HERACLES (*to Antiope*) What's happened to her?

HIPPOLYTE. Never mind what's happened to *me*. We're discussing what's going to happen to you.

HERACLES. I shall try to keep my temper.

HIPPOLYTE. The nearest frontier post is seven miles from here. It is called Pellusium. I shall give you exactly sixty minutes to get out.

HERACLES. Oh, ho! Interesting. So this is an ultimatum?

HIPPOLYTE. It is that precisely.

ANTIOPE. Oh, no, it isn't. Pellusium is delightful. You'd love it.

HERACLES. And suppose I should ignore your ultimatum?

HIPPOLYTE. Ignore it if you wish. Stay by all means; but think twice. How long can you go without eating or drinking?

HERACLES. And why, pray, do you suppose I intend foregoing those pleasant habits?

HIPPOLYTE. Because you will never be sure, will you, which dish contains the anticipated poison?

ANTIOPE. Oh, no. My lord, she has been struck by lightning.

HIPPOLYTE}
HERACLES } (*together*) You keep out of this!

HIPPOLYTE. In the same way, you will go without sleep for fear of the assassin's knife. Think it over, but not for too long. (*To Antiope*) Where is Thalestris?

HERACLES. I do not require to think it over. I intend to encroach upon your hospitality still further and stay. I can last many days without food and drink and many nights without sleep. And my men will be returning soon. When they do, I pity you. If it was your intention to introduce me to fear, you have succeeded; fear lest I lose my power of self-control and proceed to snap your insipid head from its unappetizing body.

HIPPOLYTE. Well, really, there's no need to be common. But

like father like son, I suppose. Not that I usually look like this,
I assure you. (*She turns and calls*) Thalestris.

(HIPPOLYTE *exits* L)

HERACLES. What has got into her?
ANTIOPE. Well—something has. That's why I asked you if you
would leave us. You must. It's not safe here.
HERACLES. Leave here? Leave you? Do you suppose I would?
Simply because a daft girl has threatened me?
ANTIOPE. She'll stop at nothing. She's—she's more powerful
than you know. So, please.

(HERACLES *shakes his head*)

No?
HERACLES. No.
ANTIOPE (*despondently*) No.
HERACLES. I am sorry.
ANTIOPE. Then—then, will you let me hide you?
HERACLES. No, madam—(*he smiles*) that still less.
ANTIOPE. Why not? I will give out that you have gone, and
when your friend returns . . .
HERACLES. I am the wrong size for hide-and-seek. No ordinary
wardrobe is high enough. No ordinary woman's skirt is wide
enough.
ANTIOPE. You are too proud to give me this favour.
HERACLES. Perhaps it is that, but I cannot overthrow my vices
in a twinkling.
ANTIOPE. I understand, my lord. (*She moves despondently to the
balustrade and looks off*) My lord!
HERACLES. Yes?
ANTIOPE. I believe it was—yes, I am almost sure it was. I
think it is—or is it? Just beyond the point. A ship. Could it be
one of yours returning?
HERACLES. Where? Show me, madam. (*He rushes to her side*)
ANTIOPE. No. Now it is out of sight.
HERACLES. Where? Where? Where was it?
ANTIOPE. Out there, my lord. Here, come with me. I've an
idea. Let's go to the top of the tower—the Crown Tower. One
can see for miles from there.
HERACLES. Yes, by Zeus. Hurry, hurry!

(ANTIOPE *runs to the tower door, unlocks it and exits to the tower.*
HERACLES *follows her off*)

ANTIOPE (*off in the tower*) Excuse me a minute, my lord. I have
left my scarf.

(ANTIOPE *re-enters from the tower, closes the door quietly behind her,
then locks and bolts it.*)

HIPPOLYTE *enters* L.
HIPPOBOMENE, *bewildered and frightened, follows her on*)

HIPPOLYTE (*briskly*)   Hallo, hallo; where is he? Has he gone?

(ANTIOPE *shakes her head*)

Where is he?
ANTIOPE. I have done as you suggested. He is our—prisoner.
I have locked him—out of harm's way. But will you promise . . .?
HIPPOLYTE. Promise what?
ANTIOPE. Will you promise not to injure him?
HIPPOLYTE. If he behaves himself, he's safe. Hippobomene,
take charge of the key. No, you'll be in the front line. Give it to
Thalestris. As for you, Antiope, you are still a queen and I'll
thank you to spare us a long face. It is bad for morale. So pull
yourself together.
ANTIOPE. But where will all this end? When Theseus and his
men return, there'll be the devil to pay.
HIPPOLYTE. There will, indeed. And if they want a fight,
they're going to get the fight of their lives. Themiscyra is going
to be busy these next few weeks. Now, then. Hippobomene, I
want you to collect two hundred of the biggest women in the
queendom. They will be under your personal command and you
are to be responsible for training them in the use of the double-
headed axe. You will also make arrangements to see that every
pike, spear, sword, axe and javelin in the armoury is tested, set,
polished and greased, and all the arrows, bows, clubs . . .

(THALESTRIS, *looking scared, enters* L.
DIASTA *and* ANTHEA *follow her on*)

Ah, Thalestris, where the devil have you been?

(THALESTRIS *opens her mouth to speak*)

No, don't talk: attend to your duties. You are to be in charge of
Civil Defence. Arrange to convert the Maternity Hospital into a
First Aid and Casualty Ward. Add to your staff of orderlies, get
them properly trained and put somebody responsible in charge.

(HERACLES, *in the tower, having discovered Antiope's trick, bellows and
pounds on the door*)

(*She calls to Heracles*) Quiet in there! Anthea, have that door
sandbagged. (*She turns to Diasta*) As for you, Diasta, you will be
my personal aide-de-camp. You will call me at o-five-thirty every
morning and report . . .

(HIPPOLYTE *continues with raised voice to issue orders that are,
however, rendered inaudible by the pandemonium from within the tower.
The lights dim to* BLACK-OUT. *The* FRONTCLOTH *falls and the*

curtain at the niche L *rises. A spot comes up on the niche* L *when* ZEUS
is in his place)

ZEUS. Well, now . . . Er—did I ever tell you the story of the
Monkey and the Giraffe? Yes, of course I did. That's one of the
troubles with eternity; it is so unavoidably repetitious. No wonder
we Gods envy you your mortality. Life without end. Yes, and
without surprises. How I sometimes covet your almost impene-
trable ignorance! In a God's eye there are no new visions; in a
God's ear no new tunes. Listen! To you tonight, that was a new
tune. To me? (*He shakes his head*) It has indeed ancient words.
(*He sings*)

> Oh, I'm for a tale of loving
> And I'm for a tale of war
> So make men
> And break men,
> We can always make some more.
> Aye, aye.
> That's what the girls are for.
> Remember the dead
> Were bred in a bed
> And we've plenty of beds in store,
> So gather near, my children,
> And let your voices soar
> With a melancholy tale of loving
> And a merry, merry tale of war.
> Aye, aye.
> Aye, aye.

Yes. And now—if they are ready down there . . . Now, my
children, now for the war.

The light on the niche L *fades and the gauze curtain comes down.*

SCENE 2

SCENE—*The same. A few weeks later.*
    A tremendous gong is hung upon the balustrade up C, *and a tall
ladder leans against the tower, just below a small vertical slit in the
deep wall, which is not so much a window as a viewing-point. Heracles'
club and various swords, spears, clubs and shields are set about the
courtyard. The tower door is sandbagged.*

When the FRONTCLOTH *rises, the doors* R *are open and* HIPPOBOMENE
*is standing in the doorway, looking off and drilling an unseen company
off* R. *Both in voice and bearing, she has evidently become a first-rate
company-sergeant-major. Her orders, though deafening, are so slurred
as to be barely comprehensible save to experts.*

HIPPOBOMENE. Company! Prese-ent hipe! One, two. Slope—

hipe! One, two. Company . . . Wait for it, wait for it. Company! Order—hipe. One, two, three. You're late—that woman in the front rank. Yes, you, I mean. Number seven. Keep your mind on it if you've got a mind. Company! Slope—hipe! Number seven, you're late again. Sergeant, take that woman's name. She may be a joy to her mother but she's a pain in the neck to me. Company! Stand-at—ease-as-you-were! Stand-at—ease! Company, 'shun! Pick up your dressing. Not literally, number seven.

(HIPPOLYTE *enters* L. *She is dressed in armour and carries a map. She sits on the fountain and studies the map*)

Company will move to the right in column of fours. Company, right turn. Now, heads up, bottoms in and let me see those chests come out. By the left—quick march. Left, right, left, right—number seven, you look like a miserable old man. Left, right, left, right . . .

(ANTHEA *enters* L. *She carries a jug and a loaf of black bread. She crosses to the ladder, mounts it and puts the jug and bread through the slit in the tower. Evidently she has the daily task of provisioning Heracles*)

Pick up those feet. Number seven, *dear, will* you do sargie-wargie a favour and cut your throat?

(*As* ANTHEA *is about to descend the ladder, something in the distance catches her eye. She looks for a moment longer, then hurries down the ladder and runs to Hippolyte*)

ANTHEA. Your highness! Excuse me, your highness! Theseus is back. His ships are in the harbour. They're tying up. I saw them.

HIPPOLYTE (*after a moment's further concentration on the map*) The look-out reported it to me five minutes ago.

ANTHEA. Oh, I'm sorry, ma'am. I didn't know you knew.

(ANTHEA *crosses and exits* L)

HIPPOBOMENE. Company! Break into quick time. Double march. Left, right, left, right. About—turn. One, two, three, four. About—turn. One, two, three, four. Sergeant in charge of number three platoon. That woman's losing her drawers or something. About—turn. One, two, three, four.

(HIPPOLYTE *rises and crosses to the steps* R)

Company—halt!

HIPPOLYTE. Stand them at ease.

HIPPOBOMENE. Company! Order—hipe! ,Stand-at—ease. (*She turns about herself with military precision and smartly salutes Hippolyte*)

HIPPOLYTE. Sergeant-Major.

HIPPOBOMENE. Yes, sir?

HIPPOLYTE. The enemy have arrived.

HIPPOBOMENE. Very good, sir.

HIPPOLYTE. It is time your company took up their positions. They will not move off in a body, of course. You have given them the necessary instructions?

HIPPOBOMENE. Yes, sir.

HIPPOLYTE. They are to find their way individually and keep out of sight of the harbour.

HIPPOBOMENE. Yes, sir.

HIPPOLYTE. Very good. Are your women in good heart?

HIPPOBOMENE. Yes, sir. They are a grand bunch, sir.

HIPPOLYTE. I know. I am sure they will acquit themselves like men. Good luck to you: one and all. (*She shakes Hippobomene encouragingly by the hand*)

HIPPOBOMENE (*flushing with pride*) Thank you, sir. (*She turns about*) Company! 'Shun! Yes, you too, number seven. Stand-at— ease. Stand easy.

(HIPPOBOMENE *exits* R)

(*Off*) You know your orders—no noise—break away.

(HIPPOLYTE, *with her back to the balustrade, studies her map.*
THESEUS' *head appears over the balustrade up* C. *He is beaming with pleasant anticipation.* HIPPOLYTE *turns up* C. THESEUS *quickly bobs down.* HIPPOLYTE *moves to the balustrade up* C. *As she reaches it,* THESEUS *bobs up*)

THESEUS. Boo!

HIPPOLYTE. What the devil are you doing? How in the world did you get in here?

THESEUS. Well, really! Aren't you glad to see me? (*He climbs on to the balustrade and sits on it, his legs on stage*)

HIPPOLYTE (*yelling*) Answer me! How did you get past the guards? (*She looks over the balustrade*)

THESEUS. Guards—what guards? You don't *have* guards.

HIPPOLYTE. *Evidently* we don't. Someone will be court-mar-tialled for this. (*She goes up the steps* R *and looks off*)

THESEUS. What do you mean? You were expecting me. I came as soon as your messenger arrived.

HIPPOLYTE (*turning at the top of the steps*) I was not expecting you to climb over the wall like a lunatic.

THESEUS (*jumping off the balustrade and moving down* C) Oho, did naughty ickle Hippolyte get out of bed the wong side this morning?

HIPPOLYTE. Will you kindly stop drivelling and pay attention to me?

THESEUS. Do you know, you seem to have changed somehow. You're not in the least as I remember you.

HIPPOLYTE. Possibly, but memory is not your strongest suit. (*She crosses towards him*) You received my invitation?

THESEUS. Yes.

HIPPOLYTE. And your comrades? You informed them? Are they coming?

THESEUS. They'll be delighted.

HIPPOLYTE. All of them?

THESEUS. Oh, yes. They've been on board ship now for many months. This will be their first party since leaving Greece.

HIPPOLYTE. It should be quite a party. (*She crosses below the fountain to* LC) How many are there?

THESEUS (*moving up* C) Three hundred and twenty, I'm afraid. You're *sure* that's not too much?

HIPPOLYTE. Too much? No, my dear boy, we're ready to cope with twice that number. Do you see that gong?

THESEUS. Yes.

HIPPOLYTE. It is the dinner gong. When it is sounded, you will all—be served. (*She laughs hugely*) You must excuse me, now. I have a little last-minute catering to do.

(HIPPOLYTE *exits* L. THESEUS, *slightly puzzled, looks after her.*

ANTIOPE *enters quietly* R. *She wears the belt and is white and anxious*)

ANTIOPE (*quietly*) Theseus.

THESEUS (*turning*) Hello. (*He crosses below the fountain to her*)

ANTIOPE (*urgently*) My lord, we have little time. We are on the edge of disaster—all of us, you no less than we. My sister—my sister has—changed.

THESEUS. Do you know—I thought so. What happened?

ANTIOPE. It is a deep change, deeper than I can explain. It will not last but meanwhile the mischief will have been done. We shall have betrayed ourselves, we shall have lost faith, and, if *we* sink, there may be left only a world of barbarism; a world of men, with women as their corrupted satellites. I am not rancorous at you, my lord, but where you dominate there must be degradation. In the name of equality, we shall be tricked into descending to your level. Oh, my lord, we, too, have faults, grave, ugly faults and follies, but at least—you must see this—we are not worshippers of death.

THESEUS. But what's *happened* to her—to Hippolyte?

ANTIOPE. What? She—she was struck by lightning.

THESEUS. Oh, that's nasty.

ANTIOPE. And now we have to fight.

THESEUS. I don't quite see the connexion.

ANTIOPE. Don't you understand? The Amazons have been trained for war.

THESEUS. War?

ANTIOPE. It is the first instalment of equality. You have been bidden to a feast, you and your men. But it is to be a feast of blood. (*She leads him to the balustrade up* c) When they reach the narrow road at the bottom of the valley, Hippolyte will strike that gong. At the sound of it, her troops, already hidden on the hillsides, will attack. Your men will be caught defenceless in the trap.

Theseus (*moving down* l) Well, of all the treacherous, under-hand . . . (*With the impartiality of the technician*) Though it's a pretty smart plan, I must say.

Antiope. My lord, listen to me. (*She moves down* c) I cannot have my women fight. Your goddess Hera is a fool. She has done this to frustrate Heracles, and the world of men. She will have frustrated us as well.

Theseus. Where is he—Heracles?

Antiope. A prisoner in the tower. Will you help me save him?

Theseus (*crossing to the tower door*) Of course. (*He looks around the sandbags*)

Antiope. Then you must help me stop the war.

Theseus. But how?

Antiope. There is only one way. *You* must fight *me*.

Theseus (*backing down* r) What?

Antiope (*following Theseus*) Our differences must be settled by single combat. It's not unusual. You know that.

Theseus. Oh, but I couldn't, really, I couldn't.

Antiope. Why not? Why not?

Theseus. Well, I should make mincemeat of you.

Antiope. No, no. It wouldn't be a real fight. We'll make-believe. I'll do as well as I can and you do just enough to hold me off.

Theseus. Which of us is to win?

Antiope. Well—ideally, neither of us. I thought a draw would be rather nice. Then we could make a sensible settlement. We should retain our belt and you would go home with Heracles, unharmed and free.

Theseus. It's not a bad idea.

Antiope. Will you do it?

Theseus. Yes, I will.

Antiope. Oh, you darling little thing. (*She kisses him*)

(Theseus *is delighted, then notices the belt*)

Theseus. I say, is that the famous belt?

Antiope. What? Yes. Hippolyte insisted that I wear it: today of all days! We haven't much time. I must go and dig out some armour to get into—if there's any left. I'll be back.

(Antiope *exits* l. Theseus *scratches his head, turns and surveys the tower, crosses and furtively climbs the ladder*)

Theseus (*calling sotto voce into the slit*) Heracles! Heracles, old fellow. It is I—Theseus. If you can hear me—listen. There's trouble brewing. You've got to get out of here. The Amazons have armed themselves—they want to fight. It's dotty, but they do. We may need you. You should be with us. It could be any minute now. Get yourself out. I don't know how you'll do it, but you've got to. Is there a window? What about the roof? (*He glances over his shoulder*) They're coming. (*He slips down the ladder*)

(HIPPOLYTE *enters* L, *armed with a large gong-stick*)

Hullo. What are we doing with that?
HIPPOLYTE. It is nearly dinner time. Our guests are coming up the road. (*She moves towards the gong*)
THESEUS (*intercepting her; smiling*) There is no great hurry: they have a longish walk.
HIPPOLYTE. Out of my way, young man. I wish to strike that gong. (*She takes a step forward and lifts the gong-stick*)
THESEUS. Oh, no, you don't. (*He snatches the stick from her*) Aha, aha!
HIPPOLYTE. Give me that stick.

(THESEUS *puts the stick behind his back and guards the gong*)

THESEUS. Wouldn't you like to get it!
HIPPOLYTE. Yes—and I intend to get it. (*She draws her sword and lunges at him*)
THESEUS. Oh, ho! Would you? (*He parries with the stick*)
HIPPOLYTE. I'll teach you.
THESEUS. Come on, then. Teach me.

(*They fight*)

Oho! Not bad. Not bad.
HIPPOLYTE. I'll show you I'm a match for you.
THESEUS. You will, will you? Nicely, nicely. Thrust, parry. Parry, thrust. Watch out for your legs—that's it.
HIPPOLYTE (*becoming desperate*) Oh, stop it, will you? I'm in a hurry.
THESEUS. I thought you were a match for me.
HIPPOLYTE (*growling with frustration*) Oh . . . (*She redoubles her attack, but in vain*)

(ZEUS *is heard through the loud-speakers*)

ZEUS (*off*) Well done, my dear. You have all the facility of a giraffe.
HIPPOLYTE. You keep out of this. (*She turns back to Theseus*)

(THESEUS, *taken off guard by the interruption, finds his gong-stick knocked out of his hand. He is forced to draw his sword. At the same time there is the unfamiliar sound of cracking masonry. An enormous stone, at least a hundred and fifty cubic feet of it, is being propelled inexorably from the tower and crashes with a loud thud on to the ground*

below, with a clatter of mortar and rock chips showering down with it.
It leaves a gaping hole ten feet above ground level in the tower, in which
HERACLES *is momentarily framed, flaming for vengeance*)

THESEUS. What on earth . . .?
HERACLES (*at the top of his voice*) I come! Heracles! (*He leaps down*)
THESEUS. Nice work, old fellow. Delighted to see you.

(HERACLES *seizes Theseus and Hippolyte by the wrists of their sword-arms and holding them immobile, he bellows thunderously for Antiope. His is a fury to dwarf a thunderstorm. His face, even his eyeballs are red. Every muscle of his vast body flexes involuntarily. It is the mood in which he slew his wife and Linos and several other friends. Even* HIPPOLYTE *and* THESEUS *cower*)

HERACLES (*bellowing*) Antiope! Antiope! Where is that murdering, treacherous snake? Antiope! I'll tear her into a thousand pieces. I'll tear the skin off her bones with my bare teeth. Where is she? Answer me, you, before I crack your skulls together.
HIPPOLYTE. Take your hands off me, you blasphemous oaf!
HERACLES (*forcing Hippolyte on to her knees*) Silence, you, or I'll pound you into a powder.
THESEUS. Now, calm yourself, dear boy . . .
HERACLES (*forcing Theseus to his knees*) Don't order me about, you empty-headed dwarf. (*He moves down* R, *hauling the others with him*) Where is Antiope? Do you know what she did, zany? She tricked me! Me, Heracles, like a green boy. (*He paces inconsequently all over the courtyard, dragging the others ignominiously with him*) I'll gouge her eyes out. I'll twist her head full circle on her neck. I'll . . . Where is Antiope? (*He faces front, swinging the others around*) Will no-one answer me? (*He hauls them up* L, *going over to the fountain*)
THESEUS. I'm sure she won't be long.
HERACLES (*dragging them down* R) Long, long? How long is long?
THESEUS. I don't know, but do keep cool. You know what happens when you lose your temper.
HERACLES (*swinging them round*) I never lose my temper!

(HIPPOLYTE, *with fierce concentration, desperately tries to release herself*)

(*To Hippolyte*) Stop pulling, you, or I'll murder you, too. (*He virtually notices her for the first time*) What on earth are you doing in those ridiculous clothes?
HIPPOLYTE (*indignantly*) Ridiculous? They are the same as yours, my good man.
THESEUS. That's the point, old chap. I told you. They've been training. They want to fight. The entire country's under arms.

HERACLES. Excellent! Nothing could suit me better.

HIPPOLYTE (*to Theseus*) Who told *you* that?

THESEUS. Your sister.

HIPPOLYTE. Antiope! The traitorous slut! She'll pay for that.

HERACLES (*releasing Theseus*) Oh, no, madam: I claim priority. When does the war begin?

THESEUS. It doesn't begin. That is to say, there's been a change of plans.

HERACLES }
HIPPOLYTE } (*together*) What?

THESEUS. I've arranged it with Antiope. We're going to settle everything by single combat, just she and I.

HIPPOLYTE (*struggling in vain to free herself*) You'll certainly do nothing of the kind.

HERACLES. A single combat. Better and better. I'll take your place.

THESEUS (*appalled*) Oh, no, you can't, dear chap. Not possibly. You can't.

HERACLES. I can't? Who says I can't?

HIPPOLYTE. I say so. There will be no single combat. There will . . .

HERACLES. Silence, you offal! (*He roughly gags Hippolyte's mouth with his free hand*) Theseus, are you a comrade or an enemy?

THESEUS. A comrade, but . . .

(*There is a trumpet fanfare off* L. THESEUS *moves up* C.

ANTIOPE *enters* L, *girded for the fray. She, like Hippolyte, is now in a short tunic, but the whole equipment somehow sits more incongruously upon her, partly because her helmet is a size too large, as is the mighty sword that hangs from her waist. A quiver is also attached to her. In addition, she carries a large bow and a club, which, even without the other impedimenta, would be too much for her. She hitches up her tunic at the shoulder, raises the helmet from her eyes and halts in surprise at seeing Heracles*)

ANTIOPE. Great Ashtoreth! How did *you* get out?

HERACLES (*retaining his hold on Hippolyte*) Through no help of yours, madam. I see you are ready for the fray.

ANTIOPE. We-ell . . .

HERACLES. Theseus has graciously allowed me to take his place.

ANTIOPE. What! Oh, no, that won't do at all. Really, it won't.

HERACLES. It will do very nicely, I assure you.

ANTIOPE. No, honestly! You see, your friend must have forgotten—a—a certain point. It simply wouldn't work.

HERACLES. Then we must make it work.

THESEUS. Heracles, dear fellow. She's right. I promised . . .

HERACLES. Don't "dear fellow" me! Was it you that she betrayed? Was it you she tricked into the tower?

THESEUS. No, of course. It was you. I would never have been such a . . .

HERACLES. Then it is my privilege, "dear fellow", to pound her carcase to a pulp. (*To Antiope*) On guard!

ANTIOPE. Oh, how can you be so silly!

HERACLES. On guard!

ANTIOPE. My lord, this is not good sense.

HERACLES. You may have choice of weapons. Clubs?

ANTIOPE (*impatiently*) No, no!

HERACLES. The long spear?

ANTIOPE. Don't be ridiculous!

HERACLES. The bow and arrow?

ANTIOPE. Certainly not!

HERACLES. Well, swords, then?

ANTIOPE. Oh, stop it, will you?

HERACLES. Would you prefer to wrestle?

ANTIOPE (*a light of hope in her eyes*) Yes.

HERACLES (*thinking better of it*) No. No, I'm not as silly as that. Out with your sword.

ANTIOPE (*terrified*) My lord, I can't, I can't!

HERACLES. Do you refuse to fight?

(ANTIOPE *gulps affirmatively*)

Very well, then; you shall die like a rat. (*He releases Hippolyte, seizes his club, lifts it above his head and brings it down mightily*)

(ANTIOPE *screams and barely skips aside in time.* HERACLES *follows her up* C *and corners her. This time he takes a great lateral swing.* ANTIOPE *ducks and his club hits the gong resoundingly, rending it from its moorings and sending it clanging and clattering downhill into the valley below.* HIPPOLYTE *laughs and laughs triumphantly.* THESEUS *runs to Heracles and clutches at his arm*)

THESEUS. Imbecile! *Now* look what you've done.

(HIPPOLYTE, *delighted, runs to the balustrade and looks over*)

HERACLES. What *have* I done?

THESEUS. That gong's the signal for an ambush. Our men will be trapped and massacred.

HERACLES. Then why in heaven didn't you tell me?

THESEUS. I clean forgot. After all, we *were* busy. (*He rushes to the balustrade*)

HERACLES. Oh, Zeus! Dear Zeus!

THESEUS. Look! They're swarming down the hillsides like ants. We must go and help.

(HERACLES *joins Theseus at the balustrade.* HIPPOLYTE *goes quickly up the steps* R *and grabs a sword.* THESEUS *turns and dashes to the steps* R, *but finds himself intercepted by the point of* HIPPOLYTE's *sword.* ANTIOPE *looks over the balustrade*)

HIPPOLYTE. Oh, no. You will stay here.

THESEUS. Now, really, Hippolyte. I'm in a hurry. Please don't be a bore.

HIPPOLYTE. I said you will stay here. (*She comes down the steps*)

THESEUS (*backing below the fountain*) Oh, damn it! (*He has no alternative but to fight*)

(HERACLES, *at the sound of the clashing swords, swings round on Antiope, seizes her by the wrist, draws the sword from her scabbard, releases her and tosses the sword to her.* ANTIOPE *catches it against her will*)

HERACLES (*drawing his sword*) Have at you!

(ANTIOPE *holds her weapon up ineptly in front of her, so limply that, when* HERACLES *strikes it, it flows like a lily in the wind*)

ANTIOPE (*suddenly crying out*) Stop. (*Her eyes stare in horror over Heracles' shoulder*)

(HERACLES *swings round and looks behind him.* ANTIOPE *drops her sword, picks up her skirts, forgetful that they are only a brief tunic, and bolts.* HERACLES *turns and follows her*)

HERACLES (*roaring*) Oh, you would, would you? Am I a schoolboy to fall for a trick like that?

ANTIOPE. Well you did, didn't you?

(ANTIOPE *dodges first behind Theseus, then behind Hippolyte.* HERACLES *chases her from both, then she flees into the palace* L. HERACLES *pursues her off, bellowing threats and imprecations. Meanwhile,* THESEUS *is having increasing difficulties with* HIPPOLYTE)

THESEUS. Now, do stop this. Be a sensible girl, please.

HIPPOLYTE. You can save your breath.

THESEUS. Look, I've got to get down there and help. I really don't want to hurt you, but I'll have to. Now, will you please give over?

HIPPOLYTE. No, I will not.

THESEUS. Oh, well, it can't be helped. I'm sorry. (*He lifts his sword and, holding it with both hands, brings down the flat of it heavily on to Hippolyte's helmet*)

(*There is a flash of lightning and a clap of thunder.* HIPPOLYTE *spirals to the ground, unconscious*)

(*He turns to run off* R, *but checks himself, sheathes his sword, returns anxiously to Hippolyte's side, kneels and tries to bring her round*) Darling, come to, come to; there's a good girl. Quickly, now. You know I'm in a hurry. Oh, my lord! Hippolyte. Have I hurt you? Here, take a deep breath.

(HIPPOLYTE *stirs*)

There, that's better.

HIPPOLYTE (*opening her eyes*) I don't feel at all well.
THESEUS. You will. You will soon.

(*The curtains at the niches* R *and* L *rise. Spots come up on the niches.* ZEUS *is in his place and the niche* R *is no longer empty. The bust of* HERA *has returned; but a purple shadow over one eye looks somehow rather like a contusion*)

HIPPOLYTE. Where am I? (*She sits up painfully, her head limp against his shoulder*)
THESEUS. Now, don't try to talk for a minute. (*He is relieved and absorbed in her recovery*)
ZEUS. Did you have a nice trip, my dear?
HERA. That's my business.

(*The lights on the niches go out and the curtains come down*)

THESEUS. There. Better?
HIPPOLYTE. Much better.
THESEUS. Good. You'll be all right.
HIPPOLYTE. I have a shocking head. What happened?
THESEUS. Oh, nothing, nothing. You were just taken—queer.
HIPPOLYTE. I feel as though I'd been in a battle.
THESEUS. Battle! (*He jumps to his feet*) Dear gods, I'm supposed to be in it. I'm off. It went clean out of my head.
HIPPOLYTE. You're not going to leave me?
THESEUS. I have to. I have to join the others.
HIPPOLYTE (*tottering to her feet*) You can't! I'm coming with you.
THESEUS. No! Good-bye. (*He turns to go*)

(HIPPOBOMENE *enters* R, *dusty and ragged, from the battlefield. She is limping heavily and using* DIASTA *as a crutch*)

Aha! (*He draws his sword*) On guard!

(DIASTA *screams*)

HIPPOBOMENE. Stop it! I'm wounded.
THESEUS. Oh, I beg your pardon. Long live the Greeks!

(THESEUS *dashes off* R)

HIPPOLYTE (*following Theseus in a quasi-drunken daze*) Long live the Greeks!

(HIPPOLYTE *exits* R. DIASTA *steers* HIPPOBOMENE *to the fountain and seats her*)

DIASTA. Steady. That's right. Lean on me.

(THALESTRIS *enters* L, *with bandages*)

THALESTRIS. Hippo, dearest! What is it? Are you wounded? Is it bad?

HIPPOBOMENE. Pretty bad. Some beastly little man threw a great clod of earth and caught me full in the kneecap. (*She raises her skirt and shows a wound on her left knee*)

THALESTRIS. Oh, dear. (*She kneels*) Let me bathe it. (*She does so from the fountain-pool*)

HIPPOBOMENE. Ouch!

THALESTRIS. I'm sorry.

HIPPOBOMENE. You know, they're all extremely rough down there.

(DIASTA *goes to the balustrade to watch the battle*)

THALESTRIS. Does it hurt?

HIPPOBOMENE. Hurt? If you want to know, this is my first battle and my last.

THALESTRIS. How is it going?

HIPPOBOMENE. Very badly. For some unknown reason, the gong was late. That meant the men were practically out of the gorge when we started the ructions. The result was they had time to scatter. Then they started throwing things—great boulders and rocks and stones. It was most unfair. It was as much as we could do to skip out of the way.

THALESTRIS. Men simply are not to be trusted. (*She rises from her knees*)

DIASTA. Oh, dear, it's getting worse and worse. It's all too horrible. I've never seen such a shambles. Everyone pushing and shoving.

(THALESTRIS *goes to the balustrade*)

Look! Those men are fighting like wild animals.

THALESTRIS. Where did they get the weapons from? They were supposed to be coming to a party.

(HIPPOBOMENE *rises and hobbles to the balustrade*)

HIPPOBOMENE. They took them from our girls.

THALESTRIS. How mean!

HIPPOBOMENE. Oh, they've behaved disgustingly. Whenever one of our side stumbled and fell, they calmly ran off with her weapons. Sometimes, they didn't even wait for accidents. They'd go up to our troops as cool as you please and simply wrench their arms out of their hands.

DIASTA (*puzzled*) Their *arms* out of their *hands?*

HIPPOBOMENE. Can you see that fat little man with the red cap?

DIASTA. Yes.

HIPPOBOMENE. He's got my sword.

THALESTRIS. Oh, it's a shame!

DIASTA. Look! Look there—under the olive trees. What *are* they doing to them? Look, Hippo, can you see?

THALESTRIS. Well, really!

HIPPOBOMENE. And look! Look there! Down the valley. They're running for their lives, masses of them. (*She cups her mouth and calls*) Run, girls! Run! Hurry!

DIASTA. I'm going. It's not respectable.

(DIASTA *stalks off* L)

THALESTRIS. Yes. Come, Hippo. You should be in bed.

(THALESTRIS *and* HIPPOBOMENE *exit* L. *The lights change to a sunset glow. The gauze curtains rise on the niches* R *and* L, *and spots come up on* HERA *and* ZEUS *who are in their places*)

ZEUS (*mildly*) I think it's nearly over, my dear. Woe to the vanquished.

HERA. You need not be so smug.

ZEUS. Smug?

HERA. If I could have trained them for a little longer . . .

ZEUS. No doubt. No doubt.

(*The spots on the niches fade, and the gauze curtains come down.*
HERACLES *enters* L. *His face is grave, and he carries the belt. He stands for a moment, motionless, then crosses to the balustrade and looks down on the battle.*
ANTIOPE *enters* L. *She wears a long casual garment such as Hippolyte wore when first we saw her. Her expression is unexpectedly serene.* HERACLES *turns and crosses slowly to Antiope*)

HERACLES. It is in my heart to give it to you back.

(ANTIOPE *shakes her head*)

ANTIOPE. Even if I took it, it would no longer be ours. We have betrayed it.

HERACLES. I would rather take with me another prize.

ANTIOPE. We have been corrupted. I prayed—to the wrong goddess. Yet I must stay. There is room for me in your arms but not in your world.

HERACLES. I feel the ocean already widening between us.

ANTIOPE. It was magical that we should even have crossed it at all. You—are a man, a true man. You carry the heavy past on your back, so yours is a world of fear and you must be brave.

HERACLES. You are a true woman. You carry the future under your heart, so yours is a world of hope and you must be faithful.

ANTIOPE. Two worlds.

HERACLES. Two half worlds.

ANTIOPE. But their lips can brush, have brushed.

HERACLES. Dear lips!

(*They kiss fondly*)

ANTIOPE (*gently*) Your half is waiting.

HERACLES. Yes.

ANTIOPE. And mine: or what is left of it.

HERACLES. May the gods one day join them.

ANTIOPE (*smiling*) I think your father may understand. Speak to him.

(*They kiss deeply.*
     HERACLES *exits* R. ANTIOPE *looks after him. Tears come to her eyes.*
     THALESTRIS *enters* L)

THALESTRIS (*softly*) Your highness.

(ANTIOPE *does not reply at first, for she must control herself*)

Your highness.

ANTIOPE. My name is Antiope.

THALESTRIS (*eagerly*) Does that mean—does that mean we can go back to our old habits and customs?

ANTIOPE. Yes, Thalestris.

THALESTRIS. Does it mean, now that it is all over, we really can go back to normal in every way?

ANTIOPE. We can try.

THALESTRIS. Oh. (*She puts her head on Antiope's shoulder and hugs her*)

(ANTIOPE *smiles fondly and responds.*
     THALESTRIS *exits* L. ANTIOPE *moves to the balustrade to resume her last sight of Heracles.*
     HIPPOLYTE *runs on* R)

HIPPOLYTE. Oh, darling, isn't it exciting? Theseus has asked me to go back to Athens with him. He says I'll fit in beautifully. I'm to be a spoil of war. (*She starts to unstrap some of her armour*) I must say I like the sound of it out there. From what he says, women have power without responsibility. What could be nicer? Mind you, *he* doesn't *know* they have power, but obviously they must, mustn't they? I mean, if they didn't, there would be chaos. Darling, I must hurry. (*She crosses to the entrance* L)

ANTIOPE (*looking out to sea*) You must indeed. They're weighing anchor. You may be too late.

HIPPOLYTE (*with a scream of dismay*) Oh, heaven, blast that dreadful little man. He never forgets to forget anything.

(HIPPOLYTE *scampers off* R)

(*Off; calling*) Theseus, you little ass. Theseus! Theseus!

The distant sound of voices, of orderly shouting from the harbour can be heard faintly, along with music from a lyre in a nearby room. ANTIOPE *stands looking after Heracles. From the harbour we hear again the distant cry of "Anchors aweigh, anchors aweigh", and the cry of sea-gulls as—*

the CURTAIN *falls*

FURNITURE AND PROPERTY LIST

Throughout the Play—

In niche R: Bust of Hera
In niche L: Bust of Zeus

PROLOGUE

No properties

ACT I

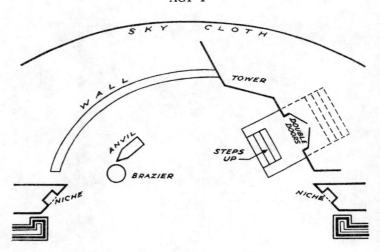

On stage—Anvil
　　　　　Brazier
　　　　　Large hinge
　　　　　Cloth
　　　　　Sledge-hammer
　　　　　Small hammer
　　　　　Long pincers
　　　　　On wall up RC: greenery growing over back of wall

Off stage—Bench (DIASTA and ANTHEA)

Personal—THESEUS: empty quiver, bow, sword
　　　　　HERACLES: sword and belt, lion-skin, gauntlets, club

78

ACT II

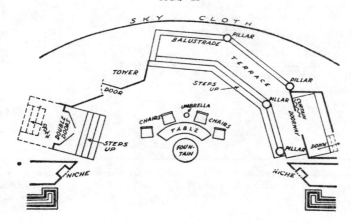

Scene 1

On stage—Table. *On it:* 4 cups, 4 plates, 2 large plates of grapes and peaches
    4 chairs. *On them:* cushions
    Large white umbrella
    On balustrade RC: wine-decanter
    On balustrade C: Heracles' and Theseus' arms and armour
    Hanging beside tower door: key
    On tower and balustrade: vine with bunches of grapes
    Curtains for doorway L

Off stage—Doll as baby, wrapped in shawls (HIPPOBOMENE)

Personal—HERACLES: scroll

Scene 2

Strike—Table
    Umbrella
    4 chairs
    Grille from tower door
    Heracles' and Theseus' arms and armour

Off stage—Tray. *On it:* bowl of fruit and grapes, decanter of wine, cup (DIASTA)

ACT III
Scene 1

Strike—Tray from fountain

Off stage—Peach (DIASTA)

Scene 2

Set—*In front of tower door:* sandbags
    Against tower under window: ladder
    On balustrade C: gong
    On terrace R *of gong:* 3 swords, 1 dagger, 1 large shield
    On terrace L *of gong:* large shield, Heracles' club

On terrace at left end: large club, small silver shield
Above doors R: 4 spears, 1 small club
Below doors R: sword, small bronze shield

Off stage—Jug, loaf of black bread (ANTHEA)
          Map (HIPPOLYTE)
          Gong stick (HIPPOLYTE)
          Bandages (THALESTRIS)
          Belt (HERACLES)

Personal—ANTIOPE: belt

Any character costumes or wigs needed in the performance of this play can be hired from Charles H. Fox Ltd, 25 Shelton Street, London W C 2

LIGHTING PLOT

Property Fittings Required—none

PROLOGUE

To open: The stage in darkness

Cue 1	As the CURTAIN rises *Bring up lights to illuminate frontcloth* *Bring up spots focused on niches* R *and* L	(page 1)
Cue 2	At end of Prologue *Fade spots on niches*	(page 5)

ACT I   Exterior

To open: Effect of bright sunlight

Cue 3	ANTIOPE: ". . . in to lunch." *Fade general lighting* *Bring up spots on niches* R *and* L	(page 30)

ACT II   SCENE 1   Exterior

To open: The stage in darkness

Cue 4	As the CURTAIN rises *Bring up lights to illuminate frontcloth* *Bring up spots on niches* R *and* L	(page 32)
Cue 5	When FRONTCLOTH rises *Bring up lights for sunlight effect* *Fade spots on niches*	(page 32)
Cue 6	THESEUS: ". . . a son of Zeus." *Dim all lights to* BLACK-OUT	(page 46)
Cue 7	Follow previous cue *Bring up spots on niches* R *and* L	(page 46)
Cue 8	ZEUS: ". . . Certainly, my dear." *Bring up general lighting for sunlight effect*	(page 47)
Cue 9	ZEUS: ". . . Am I holding things up?" *Fade spots on niches*	(page 47)

ACT II   SCENE 2   Exterior

To open: Effect of bright sunlight

No cues

ACT III   SCENE 1   Exterior

To open: All lights full up
Spots focused on niches R *and* L

Cue 10	ZEUS blows for the third time *Reduce general lighting followed by lightning flashes*	(page 55)
Cue 11	HIPPOLYTE: "My lord!" *Flash of forked lightning* *Snap in beam of light on Hippolyte*	(page 56)
Cue 12	HERA: "Oh, yes, you will." *Flash of pink lightning*	(page 57)

EFFECTS PLOT

PROLOGUE

Cue 1   Before the CURTAIN rises   (page 1)
         Music from lyre or harp
         This continues under the dialogue

Cue 2   HERA: ". . . lies asleep."   (page 1)
         Arpeggio on harp

Cue 3   HERA: "Where have you been?"   (page 2)
         Fade music

Cue 4   ZEUS: ". . . the broad Euxine . . ."   (page 5)
         Music from harp

Cue 5   ZEUS: ". . . City of Themiscyra."   (page 5)
         The music swells, augmented by the rhythmic beat of some percussion instrument

ACT I

Cue 6   THESEUS: ". . . a few arrows . . ."   (page 10)
         Harsh sound of distant trumpets

Cue 7   THESEUS: "Besides . . ."   (page 10)
         Fanfare of trumpets

Cue 8   The Palace doors open   (page 10)
         Loud fanfare of trumpets

Cue 9   ANTIOPE: "An understandable mistake."   (page 16)
         Fanfare of trumpets

ACT II
SCENE 1

Cue 10   Before the CURTAIN rises   (page 32)
          Music from lyre

Cue 11   HERA: ". . . has done to them."   (page 32)
          The music swells

Cue 12   HIPPOLYTE: ". . . is our aunt."   (page 33)
          Music ceases

SCENE 2

No cues

ACT III
SCENE 1

Cue 13   ZEUS blows second time   (page 55)
          A low rumble of thunder, followed by the sound of a rising wind

Cue 14   ZEUS blows third time   (page 55)
          Roll of thunder

Cue 15   HIPPOLYTE: "My lord!"   (page 56)
          Crash of thunder

Cue 16   HERA: "Hippolyte."   (page 56)
          Fade wind and thunder

Cue 17   HERA: "Oh, yes, you will."   (page 57)
           Peal of thunder

SCENE 2

Cue 18   HIPPOLYTE: "You keep out of this."   (page 68)
           Sound of cracking and falling masonry

Cue 19   THESEUS: "A comrade, but . . ."   (page 70)
           Trumpet fanfare

Cue 20   THESEUS strikes Hippolyte   (page 72)
           Clap of thunder

Cue 21   HIPPOLYTE: "Theseus! Theseus!"   (page 76)
           Lyre music and the cry of sea-gulls

MADE AND PRINTED IN GREAT BRITAIN BY
LATIMER TREND & COMPANY LTD PLYMOUTH
MADE IN ENGLAND